The Disciple's Handbook

The Disciple's Handbook

A Guide to Intentional Spirituality

DAVID L. HALL

WIPF & STOCK · Eugene, Oregon

THE DISCIPLE'S HANDBOOK
A Guide to Intentional Spirituality

Copyright © 2020 David L. Hall. All rights reserved. Except for brief quotations in critical publications or reviews, no part of this book may be reproduced in any manner without prior written permission from the publisher. Write: Permissions, Wipf and Stock Publishers, 199 W. 8th Ave., Suite 3, Eugene, OR 97401.

Wipf & Stock
An Imprint of Wipf and Stock Publishers
199 W. 8th Ave., Suite 3
Eugene, OR 97401

www.wipfandstock.com

PAPERBACK ISBN: 978-1-5326-9138-6
HARDCOVER ISBN: 978-1-5326-9139-3
EBOOK ISBN: 978-1-5326-9140-9

Manufactured in the U.S.A.   JANUARY 6, 2020

Touching Heaven, Changing Earth
Tangens caelum, terram mutans

"Hear my prayer, O LORD, and give ear unto my cry;
hold not thy peace at my tears:
for I am a stranger with thee, and a sojourner,
as all my fathers were."
—Ps 39:12

Contents

Introduction | ix

1. Discipleship | 1
2. Knowing Who and Whose We Are in Christ | 17
3. Spiritual Lifestyle | 25
4. Spiritual Tools | 32
5. The Church | 91

Bibliography | 101

Introduction

THE CHURCH HAS GROWN up in so many ways in the last twenty years, but has often fallen short in our calling to fulfill Christ's admonition to "obey my teachings" with a lifestyle that reflects that of our Lord (John 16:23–24). We are, nevertheless, called to continue to strive toward this end. The "charismatic" and "third wave" movements have given us a good push in the right direction with their emphasis on using the gifts of the Holy Spirit available to us. They have also reawakened us to the reality of the miraculous in the life of the church and have taken us back to the very nature of the early church. But we need even more. Christian communities need to reclaim the intentional, disciplined lifestyle that was so much a part of the early church, the church fathers, the monastic tradition, and our Reformation/Puritan forefathers. The church has lost much of this disciplined lifestyle and needs to get it back. We are, after all, called to discipleship not to membership.

Living a disciplined lifestyle will prove a challenge and, in some cases, may seem nearly impossible. We have an enemy who desperately wants us to focus our attention elsewhere. Our adversary has good reason to keep us sidetracked in our spiritual life. He knows the power that resides there, the power of Christ available to us through the practice of what has been called the Christian "disciplines," and the deeper intimacy with him they can bring us. Our natural tendency is to spiritual lethargy and sin and it is a

INTRODUCTION

struggle to put these tools into practice.[1] There is, however, a very real need to see these "disciplines" grow in the life of the church.

Being a disciple means living a life completely given over to God and his kingdom in order to effectively function according to his will. This is accomplished first through the work of the Holy Spirit in drawing us into a saving relationship with God by "grace through faith" (Eph 2:8–9). These "spiritual disciplines" do not save us but function, after salvation, as a part of the process of sanctification as we "draw near to God" (Jas 4:8). This happens through the empowering of the Holy Spirit who leads us to acts of righteousness and to become "more than conquerors" (Eph 2:10; Rom 8:37).

Why a conqueror? We are called to be like Christ as we engage the enemy for control of the world, to bring the world under Christ. So we are "more than conquerors" because we are charged to "do what I have done and even greater things will you do because I go to the Father" (John 14:12). The context of John chapters 14 to 17 is about the work of the Holy Spirit and our relationship with him. We are equipped by Christ to do all that he did and more through the empowering presence of the Holy Spirit.

This is a message that the church needs to hear again. In the West, the church has become far too influenced by the culture it finds itself in. We simply do not believe what Jesus taught in John 14:12. Just think how little you have ever heard this text preached. Try to find a commentary that will help you understand it. Very few will even try. We don't believe that we can do the things Jesus did, let alone greater things. We explain away the clear words of Christ and accept a watered-down version without power that does not require anything from us. But this is in the process of changing. The church is being drawn back into its original power, authority, and the audacity of those who take their vocation as "kings and priests" seriously (Exod 9:6; Rev 1:6; 5:10).[2] We must realize that being "in this world but not of it" means that the culture of the

---

1. Willard, *The Spirit of the Disciplines*, 105.
2. Wright, *The Day the Revolution Began*, 77, 78.

INTRODUCTION

kingdom and of this world are not compatible.[3] As Tertullian said, "What has Jerusalem to do with Athens?"[4]

Don't misunderstand here. We are called to cooperate with this world in terms of obedience to its laws, praying for its leaders, and being at peace with our neighbors (Titus 3:1; Rom 12:18). This is not a call to conqueror with the tools of this world. The goal of this book is to help you understand that all of us in God's kingdom are called to reclaim our original vocations as "kings and priests" and, in so doing, begin to function as God's warriors in the world. We must realize who we are in Christ, how God wants to use us and to use the tools that have always been part of the church but need reviving in this generation.

The Holy Spirit leads us to action but does not force us to act. We are required to act on his promptings. He also equips us to do all that is needed. First, our discipleship is accomplished through both this developing intimacy with God and through our actions on his behalf. Spiritual discipline consists of internal elements through such acts as prayer, fasting, meditation, *lectio divina* (this will be discussed later), solitude, and silence, to name a few.

The second are external such as Bible study, praise, worship, fellowship, evangelism, service/compassion, and applying the authority given to us by the Holy Spirit to heal, restore, and confront the works of the enemy.[5] This authority, which was given to us at creation, is being restored in us now.

How then do we begin to put these disciplines into practice? This question has caused no end of grief and sometimes a little despair. As a young Christian, raised in the Evangelical tradition, I was told that Bible study and prayer were essential to spiritual maturity but received little help from the church in figuring out just how I was supposed to live this out. Growing up in the '70s, most people in my church thought that a spiritual journey was something that you took with an eastern guru. Worship, on the other hand, was easy. Everyone just did it the way we did and that's

---

3. Niebuhr, *Christ and Culture*, 45.
4. Tertullian, *Prescription against Heretics*, 3:249.
5. Willard, *The Spirit of the Disciplines*, 105.

INTRODUCTION

the way it had always been done, right? You are, I hope, beginning to see why I was confused about these things called "spiritual disciplines" and what it meant to be a disciple of Jesus Christ.

In this book, I am making the following assumptions. We as Christians are supposed to be on a spiritual journey into intimacy with God. Paul says that the goal of his life was that "I may know him, and the power of his resurrection, and the fellowship of his sufferings, being made conformable unto his death" (Phil 3:10). There are also the benefits of encouragement, wisdom, and correction by the Christian community. Becoming a disciple cannot be done well, and perhaps not at all, completely outside the community of faith. Even the early monks who went into the desert to do battle with Satan were functioning in community and were not, in any real sense, "on their own."[6]

Critical to this process is recognizing that "spiritual disciplines" need to be engaged in systematically and consistently. That is, there needs to be method in our madness. We humans need the security and structure that systematic, spiritual discipline offers. If we are sporadic in our walk with Christ, we are already half-defeated. We were created as beings that need structure to make sense of our lives, and this is no less true when dealing with our spiritual life. Last, we need to write down what we learn and spend time in reflection and meditation on it. This is not as much a biblical command as it is a practical necessity that has come down to us from the spiritual journeys of others. One way to do this is to keep a journal for reflection, a journal for our Bible study, and/or a prayer journal.

The more we experience both intimacy with and obedience to the Lord, the greater the Holy Spirit can use us as agents of change in God's world. Discipleship has as its goal both knowing God (the vertical relationship) and being more and more Christ-like to those people God brings into our lives each day (horizontal relationships). The goal of the "spiritual disciplines" is for us to become what God created us to be; he has "made us kings and priests unto God" (Rev 1:6; 5:10; 1 Pet 2:9) who are called to stand

---

6. Meyendorff, *St. Gregory Palamas*, 6.

INTRODUCTION

in his presence, offer praise, and make intercession for ourselves, others, and all of his world.

This book was written to provide both a plan for an intentional, disciplined Christian lifestyle and the means for putting it into practice. The "spiritual disciplines" are critical to this end. They have, for centuries, helped Christians grow using well-tested methods for those just beginning, and have given those already on this journey additional tools to create a basic reference work for spiritual maturity.

1

Discipleship

WHAT IS DISCIPLESHIP?

"All beginnings are difficult."[1] We do not like to change the patterns of our lives. We enjoy the excitement of a momentary change but so rarely make the true lifestyle changes about which we make the obligatory resolutions that so often turn to nothing. All beginnings are indeed difficult and we rarely make it past them. One of the few systemic changes I have made began not as a result of dissatisfaction or frustration, but by the leading of the Holy Spirit. It was a gradual change; I made many wrong turns, and, as I look back on it, I have come to better understand why it came about. This is a little of what I have learned along the way.

Why should we grow?

Simply put, the Christian life is not a set of ideas to be defended but a story to be lived.[2] This new lifestyle "is not only to restore the 'image of God,' but also to attain to the, 'likeness of God' in Christ."[3]

---

1. Talmud—Mekhilta on Chemosh 19:5, section 2.
2. Willard, *The Spirit of the Disciplines*, 88.
3. Boosalis, *Orthodox Spiritual Life*, 2.

The goal of the Christian life is not to turn out fine specimens of sainthood. It is union with God, glorifying God, and enjoying God forever, fulfilling the ultimate purpose for which we were created.[4]

This is accomplished, in part, through consistent application of what Richard Foster and others have called the "spiritual disciplines,"[5] with the understanding that this is not a program to be followed for a while but a lifelong process. This assumes that it is not so much a state of being as much as steps along a journey. We all start this journey as beginners, but the journey is necessary for greater intimacy, maturity, and power in Jesus Christ. This cannot be achieved overnight, in a year, or in several but will literally take a lifetime. One of the greatest dangers to those who undertake the journey is the temptation to think that they have arrived. However much progress we see or however far we get on this journey, we need to remember the words of Thomas Merton, who reminds us that we are always beginners when it comes to the spiritual disciplines.[6]

If we want to grow in Christ, there are three essential areas of our lives that need to be brought under the control of the Holy Spirit. The first is our relationships. We must be very deliberate in our relationship with God and in our daily walk with him. This is also true of our relationships with others. Next we need to develop a disciplined prayer life. We are powerless without prayer. Lastly, we are engaged in a spiritual war. In this fight, the battlefield is our minds. What we dwell on, what we contemplate, and what we say over ourselves will be either helpful or detrimental to our spiritual growth. Some might say this sounds like fanaticism or even fundamentalism. Although both these terms are often misunderstood, that is not what I am suggesting. In much of the West, the Christian faith has been reduced to the least common denominator and, in so doing, has been stripped of the wonder, mystery, power, and glory of God. When did we so foolishly conclude that we must settle for crumbs from God when he has both

---

4. Chan, *Spiritual Theology*, 18.
5. Foster, *Celebration of Discipline*, 6.
6. Merton, *Contemplative Prayer*, 37.

promised and provided us with a feast? We have too often given in to a minimum of theological understanding and the acceptance of a corresponding cultural minimalism. We have accepted this "Spartan" ideal and are suspicious of any other expression of the Christian life, however tested and venerated in church history. We have developed a mindset, not unlike some of our political parties, totally unable to speak with those of other viewpoints even though they are brothers and sisters in Christ. The Christian lifestyle goes so much deeper than this minimalism.

We must not let ourselves be fooled into anything less than all of God's truth and all that he desires to share with us. Our faith must actually pursue the love of God in prayer, charity, and self-sacrifice. We should make the fundamentalist blush as we feast on the blessings of our God and the fanatic look indifferent as we pursue the love of the Lord. We seek, in living our lives for Christ, to become like him. We discipline ourselves so we might be steeled to the tasks he has called us to and be faithful servants of our Lord. We seek to live as he wills, to radically love people, even our enemies, to walk by faith and not by sight. There needs to be a whole new vocabulary for what we want to become and on what the church should strive to be.

Many of the old labels are inadequate and misleading. We will need other ways of telling the world that the redemption through Jesus Christ is truly good news and not the confusing and often trite message that the world associates with it. When they see and think of the church, it must have the face of Christ.

We must remember that our condition of alienation from God was removed at the cross, but the attendant habits or patterns of behavior we call sin are deep-seated in us. To bring about change, these habits, which are a direct result of our former alienation, must be replaced by healthy ones if we are to follow Paul's admonition to "renew our minds" (Rom 12:1–4). This is a lifelong process and one that, although it may have a profound effect on us, will not bring about perfection. It will, in fact, have little result if undertaken through our own effort. This is a spiritual journey and battle. It will require spiritual weapons to succeed. What is true of human intimacy is also true of our relationship with God. So, to begin this process we must recognize the following.

We are commanded by our Lord to become like him (Eph 5:1). Remaining as we are is simply not an option (Eph 2:10). Our spiritual growth, unlike our physical growth, does not happen automatically but must be undertaken deliberately and with clear purpose. Next, it is impossible to succeed in living the Christian life without the power and leading of the Holy Spirit. That is why we are called to live by faith and not by sight (Rom 8:2–4). Although this growth requires our deliberate effort, it is not magic. We cannot simply do X to get Z. The Spirit will lead us into a deeper relationship with God but not on any tit for tat basis. We have been given many tools to help us, but all that we do, although critical, does not give us progress. This is still the sovereign work of the Father.[7]

There are many ways that growth can be achieved but one of the most effective is with the guidance of someone who has been there before. Spiritual growth can be best achieved by using a mentor. This can be a tricky area and we will speak on the specifics of a mentor later. You will also need the help of the community of faith.

Lastly, we must expect opposition and struggle. G. K. Chesterton said, "Christianity has not so much been tried and found wanting, as it has been found difficult and left untried." Anyone suggesting that living the Christian life is easy has obviously never tried it. We have an enemy who does not want us to succeed. The enemy cannot hurt God directly, so he tries to do so through us. He does not want us to connect with the power of God in our increasing intimacy with him because as we grow, we become a greater and greater threat.[8]

---

7. Foster, *Celebration of Discipline*, 6.
8. Willard, *The Spirit of the Disciplines*, 6.

SPIRITUAL GROWTH

The definition of spiritual growth or maturity is to be found in the book of Hebrews. The author of Hebrews is warning Jewish Christians not to keep their focus and actions pointing toward the past. He encourages them not to focus on the "basic principles" but to become "mature" (Heb 5:12–14, ESV). The "basics" he refers to are, not surprisingly, those things that seem to dominate Christian preaching and teaching in the West. There is nothing wrong with a firm grasp of the basics, but we are called to grow into even greater spiritual maturity. Too often we have stayed safe, surrounded by our certainties (basics) which are our sure foundation—our knowledge of our place in the kingdom. We were not called, however, to live in some fortress awaiting the end, safely wrapped up in our spiritual blanket. We are called to action as part of bringing his kingdom to earth. We need to know more of how God works, be better attuned, and be obedient to the leading of the Holy Spirit.

Why must we grow spiritually?

Human beings were created for growth. On the one hand, our bodies were not created to be eternal but, as spiritual beings, we are eternal. We have an existence outside of time. We can, therefore, grow into what we were created to be. We can also, through the power of sin, regress from God. There is no middle ground here since a state of no growth is a form of stagnation. The devil's chief goal is that spiritual growth does not happen since it is the greatest threat to his kingdom. Why? As we grow in intimacy with God, we become better equipped for the warfare that is ahead of us. We are, therefore, a threat. But in that intimacy with our Lord, we are "more than conquerors" since we fight with his weapons. Weapons that the enemy cannot stand against.

Why must our spiritual life be lived out deliberately, in a disciplined lifestyle?

The church fathers tell us that our greatest failing is not remembering God, not letting our Lord be constantly and intimately involved in all of our life each and every day.[9] We allow the activities of the world, not necessarily bad in themselves, to crowd out time with the Lord. This is our nature and we would be foolish not to take that into consideration in our spiritual walk.

What does it mean to deliberately live a disciplined lifestyle?

First, we must organize our day so we are constantly reminded of God, to pray and seek his face. We must learn to make God the first priority in our calendar and daily schedule. We have often been lulled into believing that spontaneity is the true "move" of the Holy Spirit. This is, however, not what we see in either Scripture or in the life of the church. In Acts 3, Peter and John go up to the temple at the appointed time of prayer as was their regular practice. They prayed prayers from the Jewish temple ritual and later we see some of these prayers make their way into Paul's writings (Phil 2:1). Even Jesus, when reading in the synagogue, did not read any old text. Although debatable, many believe that he read from a text appointed for that day similar to the modern lectionary. There is certainly a place for spontaneous prayer but not to the exclusion of the liturgical. Part of the problem here is that we too often confuse being emotional with being devout. When it comes to prayer, it is simply bad theology to attach greater significance to one form of prayer over another. We see a good example of this in Daniel chapter 10 where Daniel is fasting and praying, but the fasting is minimal, not a total abstinence. Even so, the moment he begins to pray, God dispatches an angel with a reply. All prayer must go through the Holy Spirit to be put into a form acceptable to God (Rom 8:26) and is then presented to God from the altar in heaven

---

9. Elder Joseph, *Obedience is Life*, 130

where Jesus, acting as our high priest, presents our intercessions (Heb 4:5; 7:25). Do we really think that the form of our prayer is the key issue here?

We have been given a wonderful and varied tradition of prayer both theologically orthodox and spiritually powerful since it was inspired by the Holy Spirit. We do not have to reinvent the wheel. When we approach the throne of grace, we come into the presence of the Lord. As we commune with him, we will become more and more like him. God works both in the routine and the spontaneous, and we should exclude neither.

We must be honest with ourselves and admit that the enemy's weapons—the busyness, the anxiety of our lives, and lies about who we are in Christ—are very effective tools to distract us from time with God. Disciplined and deliberate, routine action on our part works against these distractions and can bring positive habits of mind and action into our daily life. We will not be led astray by Satan's urging us to fear, anxiety, and our supposed unworthiness if, as we are being tempted, we are in communion with God and are feeding on his presence through both the Spirit and the word.

Why is it that, despite all our efforts, we struggle for spiritual success?

The answer is that all our efforts, as important as they are, cannot succeed without the work of the Holy Spirit. When Jesus began his ministry, he received the Holy Spirit at his baptism (Matt 3:16; Luke 3:22). When he performed miracles it was through both the intimacy he had with the Father and through the power of the Holy Spirit (John 11:39–44). We have received this same Holy Spirit in order that we might live by faith and not by sight (Rom 8:1–4). It is not simply that the Holy Spirit, the agent of creation, is made available to us by Jesus' death, resurrection, and ascension, but that we are called by God to a lifestyle totally permeated by his power (John 14:12). I do not believe that the Christian life is remotely possible without the power of the Holy Spirit working in each believer and that must also include our conscious cooperation with him. We are not clever enough, powerful enough, or holy enough to defeat the power of our enemy. We have no power in ourselves but only through the Holy Spirit in the name of Jesus. And we are able to tap into the power that raised Jesus from the dead (Rom 8:11; Eph 2:6).

There is, however, no magic formula when interacting with God. He can never be manipulated but does seem to respond to his people putting a demand on him to fulfill his promises (Mal 3:19, 11). He wants us to be bold as we pray and he responds to our boldness (Ps 90). But he is in no way compelled to do so. Magic is when a person performs prescribed rituals or says the right words that compel a god or God to act according to their wishes. There is no compelling God. We are compelled to act because intimacy with our Savior and God demands it. But this growth is not a reward given to us as our wages. It is always a matter of grace on the part of God. All blessings come from a gracious God and sovereignly in his time and manner.

If we receive God's favor in our spiritual growth and it is according to his will, why do we need a mentor or spiritual elder?

I don't find fault with the desert fathers who went into the wilderness because they saw it as the realm of Satan.[10] They went to do spiritual warfare, but they seemed to do it the hard way. We, as they, must learn to be still and hear the voice of the Holy Spirit, yet we are fallible and easily led astray by our own ideas and desires. What we hear as the voice of God must be tested. The Holy Spirit does not speak in many voices but only one. God will often use our elders and mentors to confirm his word to us through their spiritual discernment. The one power that the enemy still possesses is that of deception, and we are still prone to be deceived. Therefore, we must always be cautious of our own insights. Even so, we are

---

10. Meyendorff, *St. Gregory Palamas*, 6.

still required to act, and we cannot always have complete certainty before we do.

If we are to rely on God and are required to act on the leading of the Holy Spirit in a disciplined manner, why do we need the oversight of the church?

There are several clear dangers in the spiritual life but none more treacherous than falling into spiritual pride. However intelligent we are, however skilled or pious, we are all susceptible to sin through pride. We need guidance and to be held accountable. With all of its problems, the church is the significant location of the kingdom of God and a place to keep us on track.

Why do we have trouble trusting in God?

Part of the problem is that we have been conditioned to think of God in a passive role as the Deists did. We think that we are to do all the work and we ask God to bless our efforts. This, however, is based on a faulty worldview. We were created to be like our Creator. He is actively ruling his world and we often fail to see it because we only look with the eyes of flesh and not of faith. Some people have asked me, "Why don't we see the miracles now as they did in the Bible?" That is because, unless you believe that miracles are possible, you will never see one. The problem is not the reality of God breaking into history or suspending natural laws, but that of a worldview that does not allow this as a possibility. To be able to trust in something, anything, we must first be convinced that it is possible. We must then test our data. In our time, this is difficult because so much current thinking assumes, beforehand, that we cannot trust our data in any objective way, and so the best we can hope for is some type of subjective meaning that we give to the data irrespective of any idea of objective truth. This approach, besides falling prey to all the clear arguments against skepticism, is simply unworkable. No human being can function this way. We must all assume certain things in order to simply live our lives. Certain objective truths have to be a part of our worldview in order for us to move through our daily activities. I have heard many existentialists question the objective reality of the world but I have never seen one foolish enough to run headlong into a wall. The same is true of our thoughts of God. Our thinking does not change the objective reality of who he is and what he has revealed of himself in the Scriptures. These writings provide a glimpse into his objective nature and provide us with the necessary data to develop the trust needed to be able to submit our wills and our lives to his governance. Without that trust, how can we be obedient to him?

OBEDIENCE—A LIVING FAITH

Yet, even with trust in God, there is still the matter of obedience. There is a difference between mere belief and faith. If there is a chair in the middle of a room, I can walk around it all day proclaiming my belief that it will hold my weight but it is not until I sit down that I have faith. Faith always requires commitment to take it beyond mere belief. Jesus said, "If you love me, obey my commandments" (John 14:15). To obey God is the gold standard of faith (Jas 2:14-26). Anything less and we are just playing at it.

That is not to say that we will always be successful in being obedient or that we will not occasionally sin. We will fall and we will fail as we contend with our still fallen nature. What has changed, however, is our relationship to the Father through the sacrifice of Jesus on the cross. This supreme act of love restored what was lost in the fall: intimacy and authority. The coming of the Holy Spirit brought power to live out this intimacy and authority. This is where we sometimes get confused. Before we were saved by faith, we were sinners, that is, cut off from God and powerless. After we were saved, we became the redeemed and members of God's family, the kingdom. This does not mean that we do not ever sin, but it does mean we are no longer "sinners" in this earlier sense.

As the power of God did not force us but invited us to intimacy with him, he does not compel us to live in the "Way." Rather, he provides the means, that is the Holy Spirit, for us to have the power to obey and authority to serve him. This is a partnership, as amazing as that sounds, not a dictatorship. We must act to see growth in our intimacy with him as we would to see intimacy in any relationship. We must also live out our newfound authority that is restored to us.

Trust and faith begin the journey, but it is a journey that takes time and effort on our part. Jesus came, according to 1 John 3:8b, "to destroy the works of the devil." Saving humans from hell is certainly part of that plan, but, just as certainly, it is not all of it. He will redeem all of his creation, all of his world no matter how the enemy has marred it (John 3:16). He will restore what was and is his. One of the means God uses to do this is us functioning in our proper authority before him. Those who have been redeemed have become part of an army whose purpose is to aid in redeeming the rest of creation.

HABITS OF MIND—THE PROCESS OF RENEWAL

A disciplined Christian life is a spiritual process, which engages the soul (mind, emotions, and will), the body, and the spirit in a lifelong pursuit of becoming like our Lord in every area of our lives (Eph 5:1). I am a teacher, and in education the goal is not simply to put information into students' heads but to inspire them to become lifelong learners. We seek to instill in them, through both the facts that they learn and our own example as mentors and teachers, a burning curiosity and desire to know. This is also true of the disciple. Only the object of our knowledge is the person of Jesus Christ.

We must discover a model for living out the kingdom that speaks to the needs of people now, both in and out of the church. We cannot simply rely on the models of the past. That is not to say that we cannot learn from them, or that they were wrong for their time. We must never lose such a rich deposit of wisdom as was lost for many years after the Reformation. We should not, however, fail to learn from the mistakes made. In each age of the church, people began to believe that the model they received from the past, which had served them well, was the model that God requires everyone to embrace for all time. I believe God is now revealing to the church models for disciplined Christian living for the twenty-first century. They may not be the models, methods, and structures of the past, some of which have lost touch with our world. We need dynamic yet balanced models that are theologically, spiritually, intellectually, and emotionally compelling—models that are firmly based on the revealed word of God. We must also tap into all the wisdom of those who lived out successful models before us. In each generation of the church, God raised up individuals who brought a unique vision to the kingdom and helped transform the world of their time. We need such vision for our time. As one of our bishops has said, "The most important thing you are doing, the most important thing in your life is building the kingdom of God. Commit yourself to build this church."[11]

St. Augustine called sin "missing the mark," and in many ways that is still a helpful way to understand it.[12] Sin is also like many forms of addiction. Addiction can be both physical and psychological. The addiction to cigarette smoking is an apt illustration. Many smokers have quit a thousand times, yet never seem to be quite able to give up the habit. It is not the physical addiction, however powerful, that is the main problem but the habits associated with smoking that are the hardest obstacles to overcome. To remove this addiction, smokers must change the habits associated with smoking in order to break its hold over them. To overcome sin, the power of this negative habit of mind, and the actions associated with, we must replace them with positive habits of mind and action.

"The disciplines for the spiritual life, rightly understood, are time-tested activities consciously undertaken by us as new men and women to allow our spirit ever-increasing sway over our embodied selves. They are assisting the ways of God's Kingdom to

---

11. Painter, Unpublished Sermon.
12. Augustine, *Contra Julianum* VI.

take the place of habits of sin embedded in our bodies."[13] The work of the church in forming the spiritual life of the new disciple is to train the new Christian in the practice of living in the pattern of the death and resurrection of Jesus Christ. We are further encouraged by the fact that "Christianity testifies that the past can be undone."[14] We are called to be renewed creatures, remade into our original form.

The pattern of our lives before we were saved was inherently sinful. That does not mean that we sinned all the time, but we were estranged from God and under the control of sin. When we were saved and reconciled to God in Christ, it was like the physical addiction to sin was removed but our secular environment was still there constantly reinforcing the habits of a lifetime. There was the added problem that many of us were taught that our decision of faith in Christ was the "most important decision that we would ever make" and that no amount of "good work" would make us any more saved than we are. I still believe this is a true statement. This "legal" model of salvation, however, is both incomplete and unhelpful. We were created (Genesis chapters 2–3) for intimacy with God to exercise his authority on the earth. The sin of Adam and Eve put a barrier between us and God. Salvation is meant not only to remove the barrier caused by sin, but to restore that original intimacy and authority with him. There is certainly a legal aspect to this. We are pronounced "not guilty" through Christ's death and resurrection (Rom 8:1–4). But we are also restored to a right relationship with God through Christ to lead us back to our original state with him and to live in the process of building and deepening that relationship (Phil 3:10).

It is true that our actions do not make us any more saved than when we believed, but they are critical to our growth into greater intimacy with our Lord. Jesus called all of his followers to discipleship, which means not just believing in him but also putting what he commanded into practice. Jesus said, "If you love me, you will obey what I command" (John 14:15). We must learn, then, not

---

13. Willard, *The Spirit of the Disciplines*, 19.
14. Chryssavgis, *Repentance and Confession*, 4.

how to have spirituality, something that we turn on at a particular place or time, but to be spiritual, a habit of life, and a continual state of being.[15]

Jesus introduced his disciples into the intimacy that would come in full later through his sacrifice but also gave them a temporary download of power over the works of the enemy. He sent them out to minister in the same power in which he had been ministering, functioning in an authority that would soon be restored to them (Mark 6:7).

How to Begin—Methodology

To develop the lifestyle of a disciple we must begin by recognizing the following.

We have developed a lifetime of sinful patterns and they are often hard to change.

The bad ones must not just be rejected but must be replaced with good ones. These new, good habits must be reinforced by consistent application. We cannot do this on our own. We need the empowering of the Holy Spirit, the community of the church, and a spiritual mentor to help us.

First, find a mature Christian whom you trust and who is willing to be your mentor. If you cannot find one, seek the counsel of your priest or pastor. Do not proceed with the next steps until this is accomplished. Your mentor is there as a safety net, a source of encouragement and spiritual wisdom.[16]

Set a reasonable goal or rule for one week. You might read the *Daily Light* and pray, you might do the "Morning and Evening Prayer" from the *Book of Common Prayer* or the like. Use whichever spiritual reading material or devotional tool you wish. If you are unfamiliar with the ones out there, see your priest or pastor. As Simon Chan put it, "A rule of life is not about observing a set of rules in order to make ourselves good and acceptable to God . . .

---

15. Willard, *The Spirit of the Disciplines*, 85.
16. Ware, *The Inner Kingdom*, 145.

The problem is not that we lack a rule, but that over the years we have evolved a bad one."[17]

A good way to begin is to make a chart and keep track of how you keep your rule. A key to this is that you do not go on to the next step until you have consistently kept your rule for two to three weeks. Do not move on until consistency has been achieved. These new behaviors need time and consistent application to become habits. After keeping your rule as stated above, add a little more to it. Some examples might include:

- Using a prayer rope with the Jesus Prayer
- Bible reading
- The lectionary or other reading plans
- Sacred reading
- Church fathers or other classic Christian authors

While doing this, keep a record of what you have done and consult with your mentor before moving to the next step. After these habits are well established, you will not need to keep records, but this is very helpful in the beginning.

When you have struggles with consistency, and you will, give yourself more time until you can consistently perform your rule.

Spiritual Direction—Using Your Mentor

In this relationship with your mentor, the initiative is up to you. You should consult with your mentor when you want to add, subtract, or change any element of your rule. It is alright to take off or add to your rule remembering that it is consistency of performance that is the goal. Do nothing to your rule without speaking with your mentor.[18]

---

17. Chan, *Spiritual Theology*, 190.
18. Ware, *The Inner Kingdom*, 130.

The Disciple's Handbook

Opposition—Spiritual Warfare

There will be spiritual opposition especially where prayer and any other spiritual practice is involved that draws us into greater intimacy with God.

A Note of Caution about Mentoring.

The role of a mentor is to help and guide you but not to control. I have seen this idea abused in a number of settings and by various groups. This does not mean that it should not be used but, rather, that it is important because this is an area that the enemy has always attacked. When our enemy attacks something, it is usually because he is afraid of its spiritual power. The mentor or "Spiritual Father" of the Eastern Orthodox tradition has been one of the most effective methods of spiritual growth in the history of the church. It has been used effectively in many Christian groups and is very much in vogue in business. There is also a great deal of literature both sacred and secular to attest to its worth. But that it not why it is included here. It is a safeguard to give those new to the journey a sounding board for the spiritual lessons they are learning and the things there are experiencing in the Lord. This journey is a difficult one. We have an enemy who does not want us to grow into greater intimacy with our Lord. We all need someone to help keep us grounded.[19]

C. S. Lewis made a profound statement on this matter when he said, "Mere improvement is no redemption, though redemption always improves even here and now, and will in the end improve them to a degree we cannot yet imagine. God became man to turn creatures into sons; not simply to produce better men of the old kind but to produce a new kind of man."[20] This is the end we are seeking.

---

19. Mantzarides, *Orthodox Spiritual Life*, 82.
20. Coniaris, *Philokalia*, 3.

2

Knowing Who and Whose We Are in Christ

THE PROBLEM

"Christ has won the battle of sin in your life, your enemy is defeated. Why are you trying to win by your own strength what he has already won for you?" This was a poignant question posed to our congregation by our bishop, Richard Coleman.[1] He wasn't telling us not to act but to realize a key point. We cannot win over the power of the enemy in our own strength; it is the work of the Holy Spirit. Part of our job as Christians is to grasp both "who" we are and "whose" we are. Failing to do this and, worse yet, accepting the lies about ourselves that the enemy pushes on us, can do us much harm and keep us from all we are called to be.

Bishop Coleman went on to make this clear. "Every attack of the enemy is designed to get you to move off your place of strength in the Holy Spirit."[2] If we give up our place, we are vulnerable to attack. The reason is that, as in an argument, if you agree to a premise that is untrue, your conclusions will always be suspect. I

---

1. Coleman, Unpublished Sermon, 10/8/2000.
2. Coleman, Unpublished Sermon, 10/8/2000.

like to use the sixth chapter of Romans with some additional texts which I have given the title "The Truth," since it tells us, in no uncertain terms, who and whose we are.

The Truth

- I am dead to sin. "How shall we, that are dead to sin, live any longer therein?" (Rom 6:2a).

- I have been baptized into his death. "Know ye not, that so many of us as were baptized into Jesus Christ, were baptized into his death?" (Rom 6:3).

- I was raised to new life in Christ. "Therefore we are buried with him by baptism into death: that like as Christ was raised up from the dead by the glory of the Father, even so we also should walk in newness of life" (Rom 6:4).

- Death and sin no longer have power over me. "I am come that they might have life, and that they might have it abundantly" (John 10:10b).

- My "old self" was crucified with Christ on the cross. ". . . our old man is crucified with him . . . that henceforth we shall not serve sin" (Rom 6:6).

- I have been freed from sin. "For he that is dead is freed from sin" (Rom 6:7).

- Sin and death are no longer my masters. "Now if we are dead with Christ, we believe that we shall also live with him" (Rom 6:8).

- I am dead to sin and alive to Christ. "Likewise reckon ye also yourselves to be dead indeed unto sin, but alive unto God through Jesus Christ our Lord" (Rom 6:11).

- I will not offer my body to sin but will give myself to God as an offering. "Let not sin therefore reign in your mortal body" (Rom 6:12a). ". . . present your bodies a living sacrifice, holy,

- acceptable unto God, which is your reasonable service" (Rom 12:1b).
- My body is the temple of the Holy Spirit. "... your body is the temple of the Holy Ghost which is in you"(1 Cor 6:13–20).
- I, therefore, choose to think the truth and not conform to the pattern of this world. I will act to become transformed by the renewing of my mind in Christ that I may know and do his will. "And be not conformed to this world: but be transformed by the renewing of your mind that ye may prove what is that good, and acceptable, and perfect will of God" (Rom 12:12).

It is important to note that two things are at work here. First, there is the reality of what God has done for us through the death and resurrection of our Savior Jesus Christ. Second, there are elements of our growth in Christ that require us to act in order for it to become a reality. We are called to be "transformed" as an action and duty of our lives (Rom 12:1–4). These changes, although brought about by the sovereign will of God, require our participation as noted above. God does not force us into intimacy with him. He calls us and we must respond to both acquire salvation and to progress into sanctification or intimacy with him (Eph 2:8–10). As Bishop Coleman said, "The plan of the enemy is to mar the image of God in us. God's plan is to restore his image in us and renew his relationship with us. We must be proactive in our cooperation with God's plan. Our greatest weapon is prayer directed through faith."[3]

We do not grow to maturity in Christ without the Holy Spirit. We are required to act and, however small our part is in this process of growth, it is critical. St. Augustine has said, "He who created you without you, will not justify you without you."[4] That leaves the question, how does the Holy Spirit, working with our actions, guide us to maturity? It is critical to remember that the Holy Spirit does not force his way into our lives. One of the eternal

3. Coleman, Unpublished Sermon, 6/13/2010.
4. Augustine, "Letter 169."

principles in the realm of the Spirit is that he must be invited in. He inspires, draws us to him, and communicates with us in so many ways. It is we, however, who must recognize when this is happening and act on it.

The good news is that God wants to interact with us and we can pray that he reveals the times, places, and activities where he wants to communicate with us. Even then, this does not guarantee that this will always happen. Remember, this is not magic. As Richard Foster noted in *Celebration of Discipline*, it is like a farmer sowing seed. You water it, tend it, etc., but only God gives the growth.[5] Our efforts put us into the proper position where we can hear from him. We cannot, however, manipulate God. What we can do is actively seek his face which James tells us will draw him to us (Jas 4:8). Gregory of Nyssa said, "Prayer is a heart to heart talk forever active on God's part, forever slow on ours."[6] If we seek God, he will find us.

How Do We Know?

When philosophers try to ascertain what it is we know or can know as individuals, they often come to the conclusion that all we can really know is that we, in fact, exist. Why? They have recognized that each of us lives, to a great extent, in our own heads. That is, in our consciousness or our souls: thought, emotion, and will. What many of the church fathers taught over the centuries is that the arena of the soul is where spiritual growth as well as temptation reside. But this is only part of the story.

We were created in the image of God whose very nature and being is community (Gen 1:17). We were created to have and share community with our God and with each other. All of our ethical teaching is based on how we treat each other (Lev 19:18). Even our relationship with God is predicated on this. We live in the eternal paradox of the Trinity. And like the Trinity, we are, in our very

---

5. Foster, *Celebration of Discipline*, 6.
6. Matthew the Poor, *Orthodox Prayer Life*, 22.

being, both one and many. We are also required to live with other individuals whose interior life can, at best, be only partially understood by others, all fraught with varying levels of understanding and misunderstanding. In short, we can only see ourselves and others "through a glass darkly" (1 Cor 13:12).

Our understanding of all things is, therefore, limited. Rather than leading us to despair, however, this understanding should do something altogether different. We have been changed by our individual and corporate encounter with our creator. This should lead us to both forgiveness, as we have been forgiven, and humility. It should also help us understand better why there is so much variety of beliefs and practices within the community of faith. We need certainty, consistency, and stability in our lives. This is clearly evident in our creation of dogma, ritual, and tradition. We are also called to have faith, which often leads us out of the logical safe havens of both intellect and experience. We are forced by faith into the logic of heaven, which is often in conflict with earthly logic. We have literally been changed into a different kind of being. We are not there yet but are in transition, and the spiritual reality of our lives is sometimes at odds with what we see around us. We are learning to see with new eyes, feel with new hearts, and act with new purpose and imperatives. This is what Paul is talking about when he tells us to "put on the new man" (Eph 4:24). It is a process which involves our ultimate transformation into the unique beings we were created to be.

This is why we should be both forgiving and humble. Humility in this context does not mean abasement but self-forgiveness on the one hand and an accurate appreciation of our real limitations on the other. We need to be forgiving to others because we are able to understand that everyone else is going through the same transition we are. In the book of Revelation, we are told of the glorious end we are predestined for when Jesus declares in triumph, "Behold, I make all things new" (Rev 21:5).

We are called by Christ to worship God "in spirit and in truth" (John 4:23, 34), so we strive to know, to understand, and to teach truth. We are, in fact, required to seek truth. It is vital, therefore, for us to speak the truth of what we know, carefully separating it from our own surmises and conclusions. Words matter and how we use what God has taught is important because we are called on to repeat his words after him, not to show how clever we are by coming up with what we think they mean. Our job is, rather, to proclaim the truth, not prove it. We are called on to love people into the kingdom as we live our lives in steady progress into the likeness of our king. We are not required to argue with those whose hearts have not been transformed by the Holy Spirit. When Peter tells us (1 Pet 3:15) "to always be prepared to make a defense (*apologia*)" it is not a defense of our theory of creation or why a particular political policy is better than another; there are other venues for those. Rather, our defense is for "the hope that is within us" (1 Pet 3:15). We are not called to prove truth since that is clearly the job of the Holy Spirit. And we are not called to foist ourselves on others but to speak in love to "those who inquire" (1 Pet 3:15).

How do we proceed?

We must also take seriously that we face a real enemy and his power. God's goal is clear: the redemption (1 John 3:8b) of all of his creation and the defeat of the enemy. But as we begin to be part of this process, we have to recognize the following. Satan is a defeated foe. He was vanquished on the cross and his power was crushed by Christ. We need to recognize that we have been called to be warriors of the kingdom and that God has provided us with the weapons and authority we need.

We have both offensive and defensive weapons. Our defense weapons consist of our relationship with God and our neighbors. Intimacy with God builds our spiritual strength. Such things as disciplined prayer, studying the word, obedience, faith, compassion, and forgiveness fall into this category. On the offensive side, our first tool is prayer. Prayer is acting on our relationship with God and our authority to get him involved. There is an eternal principle at work here. God builds his kingdom only in response to the prayers of his people (John 15:16). As Samuel Chadwick said, "Satan dreads nothing but prayer. His one concern is to keep the saints from praying. He fears nothing from prayerless studies, prayerless work, prayerless religion. He laughs at our toil, mocks our wisdom, but he trembles when we pray."[7] God must be asked and has promised to respond when he is.

Another weapon is speaking the truth. This includes speaking the truth about ourselves, speaking God's words after him: Scripture, words of blessing, encouragement, hope, and not least, invoking the promises of God.

Another powerful defensive weapon is "guarding the mind." This one was used extensively by the ancient church fathers, especially the monks.[8] The enemy wants to keep us off guard and to get us to question every aspect of our relationship to God and others. He will attack our thoughts, but we have a whole arsenal of weapons for defensive action. When we love our enemies and prayer for them, we thwart the enemy's plans. We are also called not to judge others or pick up offenses against them. Possibly the most powerful weapon in this fight is a disciplined lifestyle. We need to constantly, out loud, remind ourselves that we serve the King of kings and that we are dependent on him for our needs. This is an effective way to drive out the fear that is one of our enemy's most effective tools. My mother used to say to me, "You have a great memory, it's just short," which was all too true. We all must remind ourselves of these things on a regular basis. The church fathers remind us that the greatest sin is to forget God, to live our lives not contemplating how he is part of every minute of every day. His love, care, and guidance through the working of the Holy Spirit is the fuel that keeps us going.

We must also remember that in this battle, we are never alone. God empowers us through the Holy Spirit. We are part of the kingdom, the church both triumphant and militant. We cannot do any of this in our own strength but "can do all things through

---

7. From Goodreads.com, http://www.goodreads.com/author/quotes/114 8687.Samuel_Chadwick.

8. Palmer et al., *The Philokalia*, 1:23, 27.

Christ" (Phil 4:13). The goal is a simple one, to save the victims of the enemy and, in turn, plunder his camp. And the best news is, we cannot lose. His kingdom is forever.

Power of Words

Just a note on the power of words. We need to do more than just understand what is true but also to speak it. When we speak the truth to ourselves we not only reinforce it but, in a mystical way, make it real. Words have power not only in the physical realm but in the spiritual. This is partly because lies, especially those from the enemy, spoken in our thoughts and elsewhere, are directed to undermine our relationship with God. Since truth comes from the word of God, we participate in its spiritual power when we come into agreement with what God has said. When we do something as simple as open our Bibles, reading and speaking the word, we come into his presence. This is because he is in his word and it "will not return to him void" (Isa 55:10, 11). We are part of his power going into the world.

We do ourselves a disservice when, given tools for our discipleship, we fail to use them. It is like a soldier going into battle without his weapons. We expect God to meet all our needs but fail to understand that he has already equipped us with the power to apply his word for our growth and development. We are called to unite ourselves to Christ (Eph 5:1) through the Holy Spirit using these very tools. In all this we are called to action. We are certainly drawn to it by the Holy Spirit but not forced to act. We are so often lax in applying these tools and there are many others we don't even consider.

3

Spiritual Lifestyle

MORE THAN CONQUERORS: WHAT DOES IT MEAN?

WE ARE NOT CALLED just to do battle but to conquer. We are both called and equipped to this task in service to Christ. We are called to a warfare that will have its defeats and setbacks but whose victory is certain. The kingdom of God will prevail and so will we as part of it. The question then is, how do we become "more than conquerors" (Rom 8:37, NIV)?

First we must know our enemy as mentioned above. It is often the case that we either do not know the nature of our enemy or that we have an exaggerated view of his capabilities. One of the main reasons that Jesus came was to "destroy the works of the devil" (1 John 3:8b). We are called to continue in the work of the kingdom until all is put under our Lord's feet (John 14:12; 1 Cor 15:25). We are here to manifest the kingdom to this world (1 Pet 2:9). Once we understand this, then we need to understand how our enemy works so we are prepared to do what we are called to. It is sometimes mistakenly thought that spiritual warfare is either the work of specialists, such as an exorcist, or not a very important work of the church. These ideas are both naïve and wrong. Whether we like it or not, we have an enemy and we are in a war. Not thinking about it does not make it go away. So our first task is to know our enemy and how he makes war.

At this point we could look at all the tools that he uses in his war on us but that would only make him seem more formidable than he is. Rather, we will look at the tools that we have to put him to flight. One of our most powerful tools is prayer. I will not go into any detail on prayer here but will refer you to the many places in this book dedicated to that subject. We were created to be in an intimate relationship with God, and anything that draws us closer to God is a defeat for our enemy. So, such things as obedience, faith, compassion, forgiveness, and consistency are powerful tools in this warfare. I would suggest that prayer is one of our most powerful weapons, but there are a whole host of others that also need to be cultivated. This is all part of the process we call "sanctification."

The ancient church fathers tell that the mind is the main battle ground, and it is here we will begin.[1] The mind is where the enemy aims his temptation, and we need to not only fight off his insinuations but fill our minds with the things of God. Things such as the word of God, contemplation of God, prayer, holy reading (*lectio divina*), and study are all part of this process. With the veil lifted (2 Cor 4:4), we are now able to understand more and more the true import of God's word. This does not mean that we will instantly understand all things in the Scriptures, but we will be growing in our understanding since we are now pointed in the right direction with the blinders off.

The second area we must consider is the will. It is not enough to know the truth if we fail to act on it. To know what is right and not to do it is a sin (Jas 4:17). This includes what we do, what we say, and even the attitudes with which we do and say them. When we act on the truth, such as Jesus' command that we love each other, it both does the will of our Father and reinforces our relationship with him. We must also speak the truth. This does not mean simply to not lie to one another but includes such things as blessings rather than cursing, saying what is true about ourselves

---

1. Boosalis, *Orthodox Spiritual Life*, 57.

and our relationship to God, and his promises to us. The spoken word has spiritual power that should never be underestimated (Prov 18:21). It is spiritual life or death for us.

Next, there is what the monks referred to as "guarding the mind."[2] The enemy is determined that we not act in a Christlike fashion using the power that is ours through the indwelling of the Holy Spirit. He wants us to be weak, afraid, and timid. We, on the other hand, as this chapter suggests, are to be "more than conquerors." But to live this out, we must continually remind ourselves of these truths since our adversary will certainly and continuously try to tell us that we are wrong.

I do not include the emotions last because they are unimportant. On the contrary, they are a critical part of who we are and were given to us by God. We both act from emotion and our emotions can come from how we act. It is true that emotion can place us in conflict with our reason and, at times, create quite a balancing act internally. There is simply no formula for how to resolve this. We do know, however, some things about how our emotions operate.

We cannot always control how we feel, and there are times when we must overcome emotions that come unbidden. That is why, when the Bible speaks of love, it is mostly a call for action. When Jesus calls us to love our enemies, he is not calling on us to feel a certain way but rather to act in love toward another who has not acted that way toward us. This is an act of the will on our part and not of emotion. Some people have objected that acting in love without the attendant emotion is hypocrisy, but this is short sighted. The Bible does not require us to feel a positive emotion for our enemies but to treat them as we would want to be treated. We cannot prevent someone considering themselves our enemy but we cannot reciprocate without forfeiting our claim to follow Christ (1 John 2:1). I do not suggest that this is easy to do, but do it we must. That is one of the reasons we find so many examples of praying for our enemies in the works of the church fathers. This was a regular part of the liturgy and has even come down to us in

---

2. Boosalis, *Orthodox Spiritual Life*, 147.

the *Book of Common Prayer*.[3] One church father has said that our salvation is intimately tied up with how we treat our neighbors.[4] Being a disciple of Jesus Christ is totally wrapped up in our treatment of our fellow human beings, whether friends or enemies.

Growing up in the Protestant faith, the use of the body was not often spoken of except in terms of ethical behavior. We were not taught anything about the body in our spiritual development. We are charged in Scripture with both caring for our bodies, which were given to us to be the temple of God, as well as controlling our passions, which can draw us away from our intimacy with him (Heb 3:12–14). We are tasked with its care and feeding on the one hand but given instructions regarding times of fasting and privation so that its needs do not control the rest of who we are. We are even, in many traditions, taught about postures to be adopted in certain circumstances. Although my Protestant friends sometimes have difficulty with this, they are often unaware that they do the same sorts of things found in more liturgical traditions. We heed admonitions, especially in the psalms, to bow our heads and even lower or close our eyes in prayer (Isa 58:5). Yet we do not see any need to kneel, stand, or prostrate ourselves as encouraged in other parts of Scripture (Ps 95:6; Neh 9:5; Ezek 44:15; Isa 49:7). We sometimes do these actions without knowing why. These actions of the body do, when understood, affect our spiritual life. All those I have mentioned are used, to a great extent, to show honor and reverence to God. These are things you do in the presence of a king. The act of showing respect or homage to our king, if done with that intention, can have a powerful effect on us. They can reinforce in us the realization that we are not our own but have been bought with a price; that we have a king and are part of his kingdom (1 Cor 6:20; 7:23). These are no mere rituals. By these actions, we proclaim with our bodies what we profess with our heart, mind, and lips—that we belong to the kingdom of God and his absolute sovereignty in it.

---

3. *Book of Common Prayer*, 279.
4. Boosalis, *Orthodox Spiritual Life*, 147

The truth regularly and consistently applied to living as a righteous warrior in the service of the king should, therefore, show in our behavior. We are called to hear the voice of the king, obey his commandments, to live and die for him, and to put his kingdom first in all things. This is not a light thing that we take on ourselves since it has implications for every area of our existence.

We must also find the power of God in the work of the Holy Spirit. Christians do not need, nor do we use, what the world calls power. Our tools for change are prayer, worship, compassion, and the truth, to name a few. God is in the process of bringing about the final resolution to the world that he has planned. He uses our free choices but also directly intervenes in our world and this is in response to our prayers. Those things that much of our world calls impossible are not so for him. We have been given many tools to affect the world around us, but none is more powerful than prayer. This is because prayer is our direct link to God, through our relationship won for us by Christ on the cross. God takes our requests and our actions and works them into his plan. A plan that cannot fail to achieve the ends that he has ordained for it. We cannot always see how all this can happen, yet it does even while we retain the freedom he created us for. The fact is that it happened, is happening, and will happen according to his will without, in any way, destroying this freedom is wonderful and beyond any human comprehension.

The Spiritual Warrior's Lifestyle

The enemy cannot hurt God but tries to do so by hurting us. His main attacks come via the mind through thoughts and insinuations, especially those that attempt to make us doubt our renewed relationship and our position in God's kingdom and his provision for our lives.

To combat the attacks of the enemy, we must continually remember God and what he has done for us in Jesus Christ. We must remind ourselves of this daily until this truth is in every breath we take, the truth of who we are and what God has equipped us to do.

We must make this part of a disciplined, warrior lifestyle with the emphasis on becoming like our Savior.

Along with a disciplined lifestyle, we must continually strive to know God. This is the meaning of the term "theologian." Evagrios of Pontus said, "If you are a theologian, you will pray truly. And if you pray truly, you are a theologian." Theologian, in this context, means one who is actively and consciously participating in or perceptive of the realities of the divine world—the realization of spiritual knowledge.[5]

Learning to be "more than conquerors" is not for some special elite. It is our job as Christians and we are tasked to fight, at times to suffer, and at times to die. Yet we are in the only army in the history of the world whose mission is saving the victims of its enemy since he is already defeated. Our job is to plunder his camp.

A Note on Power

The world's idea of power is as wrong as it can be. It begins with coercion, that is, getting people to do what it wants them to do regardless of whether they want to or not. Many tools can be applied to make this happen. Some are subtle, some crude, and some hidden. The savvy players seem to pull it off without anyone even knowing. Yet, however clever this appears, it must always come at a loss of humanity. Besides, and this is the critical part, it is all futile. This is not an open game where all who want to can play. This is, in reality, a rigged game that has already been played and won.

This does not mean that we are prohibited from engaging, as citizens of our respective countries, in its political life. It does, however, mean that we acknowledge that political gains do not equate to eternal ones. There is an ebb and flow to all political events but there is a sure and preordained march to the kingdom to God's ultimate victory. It is critical, therefore, that we do not too closely align ourselves to any political entity. It is critical that we, however much or little we involve ourselves in the political

---

5. Palmer et al., *The Philokalia*, 1:367.

process, do not sacrifice our integrity and holiness for ephemeral political "gains." Our trust must be in God, not in the "arm of flesh" (1 Chr 32:8; Pss 118:9; 146:3).

We are soldiers of the king, and as such we should be trained and equipped for the job. We must know how to fight, and we must always remember that this war has already been won. We are given the privilege of fighting and, if we fall, we know that God will raise up others who will continue the fight. We cannot be defeated. The kingdom of God is forever.

4

Spiritual Tools

SPIRITUAL DISCIPLINES

The following is a list of spiritual disciplines—but it is not intended to be exhaustive. Many other activities aid in our spiritual growth, and there are just too many to include here. Those listed below represent the foundation stones of the others.

- Study—A regular course of intellectual and spiritual reading, classes, etc.
- Service—Regular service within both community and/or church.
- Sacrifice—Offerings above and beyond the tithe in both time and resources.
- Prayer—Daily office or other devotionals.
- Worship—Regular attendance at worship and/or the daily office.
- Fellowship—Regular attendance at church fellowship and outside of church activities.
- Contemplation—Lectio divina, the Jesus Prayer, prayer ropes, retreats, etc.

- Solitude and Silence—Retreats both formal and ad hoc.
- Fasting—Weekly (Wed. and Fri.) and during Lent as able.

Study

I have always been impressed by the fact that Paul does not call us to only an emotional response to the gospel but to an intellectual one as well (Rom 11:33; 1 Cor 13:2; 2 Cor 4:6; Phil 1:9; Col 1:10; 1 Tim 2:4; Tit 1:1). This is sometimes a problem since many have been raised on a gospel that called us to either an emotional salvation experience or an intellectual assent. Both tend to mask the reality that salvation is a total commitment of all that we are: mind, emotions, will, body, and spirit. But the intellect is certainly involved in both the process of salvation and sanctification. Paul tells us that salvation comes through hearing the word of God (Rom 10:17). One of the best ways to involve the intellect in spiritual growth is through the study of Scripture. This section will help to address this use of the mind.

One of the keys in the use of the intellect is to understand that people do not think with the faculty of reason by itself. A person cannot turn off their emotions, the things that have happened to them in their life, the things that they have thought of before, or the conditions under which they must do their thinking. The use of the mind is part and parcel of the whole person. Spiritual maturity, therefore, must take place in more than just our spirit. It must take place in the whole person. In Deuteronomy 6:5 the people of Israel are enjoined to "love the Lord your God with all your heart and with all your soul and with all your strength." They were called to a devotion to God that took into account their whole being. We are called to no less.

Study will help in our effort to pray by arousing our forgotten powers, by strengthening and invigorating us. In this vein, Father Isaias instructs us: "When you arise in the morning, before you begin your work, study the words of God. When you have the words of God as your constant companion, you will not be preoccupied with worldly matters, you will not be troubled, you will not sin."[1] We are also told that "the profuse source that the Holy Spirit draws upon to supply the student with material for meditation is the Bible. The Bible is indeed the great school in which there is no end of lessons."[2]

Study requires an organized approach to the content of the Bible. To that end, it is critical that we apply our cognitive skills to understanding all that it has for us. A key skill in studying the Bible is note-taking. The ASA type of note-taking was one of the many forms used in my classes over the years and was easily the most effective.

There are many ways through which the Bible can be studied. The ASA method proved very effective because it is based on the Cornell note-taking system. It is a way to understand and organize your thoughts on the text of the Bible. This book is not designed to teach you all the many excellent methods available for this task or even to recommend one over another. There are many excellent books on this subject. The ASA method is, however, a good starting place and is compatible with several digital platforms which employ Cornell note-taking templates. Along with any method you use, there are certain tools necessary for the task. You will need a good study Bible, Bible dictionary, and introductions to the New and Old Testaments. These are important tools to have on hand. There are also a myriad of online resources for this purpose.

However sophisticated or basic your efforts are, remember that when you open the Bible, you come into the presence of its author. Bible study can be much like prayer or worship in that you open yourself up to hearing from God, being taught, encouraged, and comforted. Coming into his presence is never a mistake.

---

1. Monk Moses, "Prayer as an Important Aspect."
2. Matthew the Poor, *Orthodox Prayer*, 50.

Spiritual Tools

ASA Bible Study Note-Taking

Good note-taking is a habit which, once acquired, will greatly benefit you in your understanding and retention of the biblical text. There are several different note-taking styles, and no one is essentially better than another. Use the one that suits your style of learning best. The important aspect of biblical note taking has to do with how you analyze, synthesize, and apply information from the text. The standard three-ring binder works best for this method, but you can also effectively use a digital format. As you expand your understanding or add insights from other sources, you will be able to expand your note base without changing to a new notebook.

Analysis Synthesis Application Method

The Analysis/Synthesis/Application Method is based on a process of thought that begins with Analysis (separating something into its component parts in order to study it), Synthesis (recombining those parts to form a new whole), and Application (taking the truths discovered from this process and seeing how they relate to the question of living our lives in Christ).

Take your three-ring binder filled with standard lined paper and draw a vertical line about 1/3 into the left-hand page. On the right-hand page, write your notes from your Bible reading or devotional. The topics below can help you organize this information.

Nature of God

- Holiness—God's system of right and wrong, of which he is the prime example.
- Justice—God must punish evil and reward good which naturally follows from his holiness.
- Goodness

- Benevolence—God's positive regard toward all of his creation
- Love—God's positive regard toward humans, his special creation
- Mercy—Reduction or lessening of punishment
- Grace—No punishment and no imputation of guilt: also referred to as "unmerited favor."

Human nature—Who are we?

- Relationship between God and man
- Relationship between man and man

Summary of what you have learned

The center column is the place for synthesis. In the synthesis process, you are attempting to see how information obtained in the analysis phase relates to one another and with the great questions posed by the Bible such as, Who are we? Why are we here? Who is God? What should our relationship be to him? etc.

Application to our lives should be recorded in the facing page. On this page record what you have learned from the text using questions such as:

- How can I apply this to me? To my society? To the world as a whole?
- So what? That is: What do I gain if I apply this? What may I lose if I fail to apply this?
- Where do I go from here?

Service

It takes an exercise of our wills to put these tools of spiritual discipline to work aiding us to continually keep our eyes on Jesus. Developing intimacy with God is not something that just happens. We must desire it and act on that desire. This does not mean that we are not being drawn by the Holy Spirit but, as mentioned earlier, not forced.

There are many reasons for service, but the most compelling is God's command to love our neighbor (Lev 19:18). The biblical concept of "love," as mentioned above, has to do with how we treat each other. You can know that someone loves you by the loving manner in which you are treated. With this in mind, service to others has never been an optional activity in the history of God's people. In Jesus' teaching on the greatest commandment, he quotes Deuteronomy 6:4 as the greatest commandment with Leviticus 19:18 as the second greatest (Matt 22:38–40; Luke 10:27, 28). This is clarified even more in 1 John 2:16–18 (NIV): "This is how we know what love is: Jesus Christ laid down his life for us. And we ought to lay down our lives for our brothers. If anyone has material possessions and sees his brother in need but has no pity on him, how can the love of God be in him? Dear children, let us not love with words or tongue but with actions and in truth."

It is not important what kind of service we are called to; it is only important that we respond to that call and apply ourselves as if we were serving Jesus himself since, in fact, we are. Painting a Habitat house is not intrinsically nobler than cleaning the church toilets or cutting someone's grass. All service in the name of Christ and for the benefit of others is blessed. The key here is to get involved and use the gifts given to you to work for the kingdom (Col 3:23).

Prayer

Prayer is not just asking for our own needs. God wants us to ask for our needs, but the essence of this spiritual discipline involves both intimacy with our creator and the process that he uses to work his will in the world. "God does nothing but in answer to prayer."[3] To be sure, he can and does act in other ways but, when we came into his kingdom, we became part of the process of reclaiming this world. It rightfully belongs to our Lord. Prayer is one of the most effective tools God has given us in this process to bring about his dominion on the earth and we are called to be bold in its use.

Prayer Notes

WHY SHOULD WE PRAY?

We ought to pray because God purposes to use our prayers to bring about his will. God promised to answer our prayers and sent Jesus so we could have the privilege of coming into his presence so that our prayers could be heard (John 14:12–14; Heb 6:19).

God told us how to get things done in his kingdom: pray! God always purposes our greatest good, and he has chosen prayer as the means to get it to us (Jer 29:11). We don't know why this is, but the Scriptures make it clear that it is. I have often heard it said, "Prayer doesn't change things, prayer changes us." This implies that all prayer does is make us truly conform to the will of God and nothing else. This is only partially true. Prayer certainly changes us as we grow in intimacy with God, but it also makes things happen. The more we see him answer our prayers the greater our boldness in coming to him. His answers also encourage and strengthen us into spiritual maturity.

HOW DOES PRAYER WORK?

Jesus is our high priest and is in constant intercession for us with God the Father in the heavenly tabernacle (Heb 7:25). Jesus stands in the gap between God and us. We must learn to get in the gap with him as we intercede for ourselves and others. In times of

---

3. Olson, *John Wesley's "A Plain Account,"* 50/1525.

prayer, we obtain unique authority from God to bring the power of the Holy Spirit onto the ministry of the church. The world is dependent on us to intercede for it and the secret is: keep praying! The world says we are crazy, that God doesn't answer prayers, and that we are acting like fanatics by thinking that it does. Ignore the world and keep praying! We must, at times, come to the end of our resources so we can truly see our utter dependence on him and allow him to work through us.

What are the hindrances to prayer?

The plan of Satan is that we do not connect with God. As our intimacy with God grows, we become better vehicles for his power. We wrestle with principalities and powers that actively desire that we do not pray. Prayer is not a game; it's hard work. As St. Silouan the Athonite tells us, "Everyone who would follow our Lord Jesus Christ is engaged in spiritual warfare."[4] Prayer is not an optional activity in the Christian life, it practically defines it.

How are we to approach God?

Don't be afraid to ask for the little things since God is part of our whole life, not just the part that we think of as "spiritual." Don't, however, be satisfied with just the little things. We are called to go boldly into the presence of God (Heb 4:16). Prayer can literally do anything. The only limitation to prayer is the limit of God's power, and we know that his power has no limits.

How do we get started?

The best way to get started is to start small; but start. Even baby steps are helpful in prayer. After all, remember that everyone struggles in prayer. There are no hard and fast rules for prayer.

---

4. Matthew the Poor, *Orthodox Prayer Life*, 50

The Holy Spirit directs prayer, and the Bible helps us by providing principles and examples to aid in prayer.

It is critically important to organize our time to make room for prayer. Make appointments for prayer in your calendar or daily planner as you would for any other important event in your life. Make prayer every bit as important as a trip to the doctor or a meeting with your boss.

How does the Bible help our prayer?

The Bible tells us in Romans 12:2 and Ephesians 4:23 that we are to renew our minds and to set them on things above. Some ways to do this include studying God's word and committing it to memory. We should learn from the advertising industry that we humans are affected by what we allow to come into our minds over and over again (Phil 3:19; Col 3:2; 1 Pet 1:13). Our new attitude of mind is an important aid to prayer, as Peter tells us, "Be sober, be vigilant; because your adversary the devil walks about like a roaring lion, seeking whom he may devour" (1 Pet 5:8).

Try using the "lectio divina." This type of meditating on the word helps set our minds and hearts on God and brings us into his peace. (See below.)

What is the relationship between prayer and praise?

Prayer and praise take us outside ourselves and into the presence of God. Prayer and praise get the will of God into action and bring down the blessings and power of God. Prayer is not an option; God commands it (Col 4:2). God also commands praise. All the things of God, such as praise, the sacraments, praying, singing, etc. are hateful to our enemy (Heb 13:15). Add praise to your prayer life and see what God will do.

Spiritual Tools

What is the Place of the Trinity in Prayer? (The Prayer Conspiracy)

Today we hear of so called "conspiracy theories" which may or may not be true. There is one conspiracy that the Bible makes clear is always at work in the church. That is the prayer conspiracy. Paul tells us that since we do not know how to pray (Rom 8:26, 27), the Holy Spirit must take our prayers and put them into a form acceptable to God. Those prayers then go to the altar in heaven where they are offered to God the Father through our great high priest, Jesus (Heb 4:14,15; 7:25). Since Jesus tells us that the Father always hears his prayers (John 11:41, 42), we know that we have what we pray for. Jesus also promised that he would do whatever we asked of him (John 14:13, 14). This is the great prayer conspiracy. The Trinity of God the Son, God the Father, and God the Holy Spirit have conspired and are conspiring to answer our prayers and we are the only ones who can hinder this process by not praying.

Prayer Disciplines

Morning and Evening Prayer

The morning and evening prayer discipline that follows is based on both the *Book of Common Prayer*, the liturgy of prayer found in Eastern Orthodox churches, as well as other sources in the history of the church. The minimal practice in church history was to pray at the beginning and end of each day. If you use this prayer office, you need to keep in mind that these prayers are here as a guide. Feel free to substitute other prayers as needed.

Prayer Upon Waking

Lord, you have given me the gift of a new day. So work in me that what I do today might make a difference in my world. You delight in blessing me and making me more than a conqueror, so surround me, I pray, with your power and your favor. Let me never forget that you are the Lord of this world and I can do all things through Christ who strengthens me. Because of your great love for me and the power of your Holy Spirit, I will fear no enemy. May your name be lifted up and glorified in all the world, through Jesus Christ, our Lord. Amen.

or
Lord Jesus, grant me
wisdom to live this day as if it were my last;
strength to do all that I must;
courage to do all that I should;
and humility to acknowledge that
I can do nothing without you.
In each moment, let me remember you;
praise and honor you;
contemplate your love and mercy;
and wonder at your loving kindness
to one who deserves it least.
Let me love as I am loved;
forgive as I am forgiven,
ever seeking to become like my savior.
Let me live this day eagerly
awaiting your return.
Come quickly, Lord Jesus. Amen.

Morning Prayer

"But thanks be to God! He gives us the victory through the Lord Jesus Christ" (1 Cor 15:57).

"Calm me, O Lord, as you stilled the storm
Still me O Lord, keep me from harm
Let all the tumult within me cease
Enfold me Lord in your peace."[5]

---

5. Adam, *Edge of Glory*, 70.

Spiritual Tools

"In the same way, the Spirit helps us in our weakness. We do not know what we ought to pray for, but the Spirit himself intercedes for us with groans that words cannot express" (Rom 8:26, 27).

We pray for the salvation and good of our enemies and those who wish to do us harm; and for anyone we have injured or offended.

"Most merciful God, we confess that we have sinned against you in thought, word and deed, by what we have done, and by what we have left undone. We have not loved you with our whole heart; we have not loved our neighbors as ourselves. We are truly sorry and we humbly repent. For the sake of your Son Jesus Christ, have mercy on us and forgive us; that we may delight in your will, and walk in your ways to the glory of your Name. Amen."[6]

"Almighty God have mercy on us, forgive us all our sins through our Lord Jesus Christ, strengthen us in all goodness, and by the power of the Holy Spirit keep us in eternal life. Amen."[7]

"If you abide in my word, you are truly my disciples, and you will know the truth, and the truth will set you free" (John 8:31, 32).

"Submit yourselves therefore to God. Resist the devil, and he will flee from you. Draw near to God, and he will draw near to you. Humble yourselves before the Lord, and he will exalt you" (Jas 4:7–8, 10).

"God, you have made of one blood all the peoples of the earth, and sent your blessed Son to preach peace to those who are far off and to those who are near: Grant that people everywhere may seek after you and find you; bring the nations into your fold; pour out your Spirit upon all flesh; and hasten the coming of your kingdom; through Jesus Christ our Lord. Amen."[8]

---

6. *Book of Common Prayer*, 360.
7. *Book of Common Prayer*, 360.
8. *Book of Common Prayer*, 257.

"May the Spirit of God dwell in us; may his love reside in us. Make our hearts pure that we might see him, that he might sow in us the seed of reflection upon his mighty power and wonder at his eternal majesty. Help us to weed out from our souls the undergrowth of wrong desires and the thorns and tares of bad habits to the glory of his name. Amen."[9]

Evening Prayer

"The Cross between me and all ill
The Cross to foil the devil's skill
The Cross between me and all harm
The Cross to foil all evil's charm."[10]

"Do not let your hearts be troubled. Trust in God; trust also in me. In my house are many rooms; if it were not so, I would have told you. I am going there to prepare a place for you. And if I go and prepare a place for you, I will come back and take you with me that you also may be where I am" (John 14:1–3).

"Most merciful God, we confess that we have sinned against you in thought, word and deed, by what we have done, and by what we have left undone. We have not loved you with our whole heart; we have not loved our neighbors as ourselves. We are truly sorry and we humbly repent. For the sake of your Son Jesus Christ, have mercy on us and forgive us; that we may delight in your will, and walk in your ways to the glory of your Name. Amen."[11]

"Almighty God have mercy on us, forgive us all our sins through our Lord Jesus Christ, strengthen us in all goodness, and by the power of the Holy Spirit keep us in eternal life. Amen."[12]

---

9. Brock, *Syriac Fathers on Prayer*, 21–22.
10. Adam, *Edge of Glory*, 70.
11. *Book of Common Prayer*, 360.
12. *Book of Common Prayer*, 360.

Spiritual Tools

"Therefore, there is now no condemnation for those who are in Christ Jesus, because through Christ Jesus the Law of the Spirit of Life set me free from the law of sin and death" (Rom 8:1, 2).

Thank you, Father, that you sent your Son Jesus to redeem mankind and defeat the works of the devil. Our enemy is a defeated foe and we have been made joint heirs with Christ in your kingdom. We acknowledge that we can only live the life you desire of us through the power of the Holy Spirit. Help us not to focus on our occasional failures but strive each day to bring our thoughts, attitudes, and actions into conformity with your Spirit through the renewing of our minds. Help us to so order our lives that we imitate your divine order. Help us deliberately fill our every thought with praise and prayer so we may continually come into your presence. Amen.

"The reason the Son of God appeared was to destroy the works of the devil" (1 John 3:8b).

"For the weapons of our warfare are not of the flesh but have divine power to destroy strongholds. We destroy arguments and every lofty opinion raised against the knowledge of God, and take every thought captive to obey Christ" (2 Cor 10:4, 5).

Look down, Father, from your throne in heaven. Shine your everlasting light into my heart and let your presence dispel the shadows of evil. Keep me safe from the powers of evil, cradled in the strength of your arms. This night, grant me your peace, the peace that passes all understanding. Amen.

Prayers During the Day—The Little Offices

The "Little Offices," which are part of the monastic prayers below, can be added to morning and evening prayer as you build your personal prayer discipline.

10:00 a.m. (Terce)

"Trust in the Lord with all your heart; do not depend on your own understanding. Seek his will in all you do, and he will show you which path to take" (Prov 3:5–6).

We pray for the salvation and good of our enemies and those who wish to do us harm; and for anyone we have injured or offended.

"But the fruit of the Spirit is love, joy, peace, patience, kindness, goodness, faithfulness, gentleness, self-control; against such things there is no law" (Gal 5:22, 23).

"I believe in God the Father Almighty,
Maker of heaven and earth;
And in Jesus Christ his only Son, our Lord;
who was conceived by the Holy Ghost,
born of the Virgin Mary,
suffered under Pontius Pilate,
was crucified, dead, and buried;
he descended into hell;
the third day he rose again from the dead;
he ascended into heaven,
and sitteth on the right hand of
God the Father Almighty;
from thence he shall come to judge
the quick and the dead.
I believe in the Holy Ghost;
the holy Catholic Church;
the communion of the saints;
the forgiveness of sins;
the resurrection of the body;
and the life everlasting. Amen."[13]

"I heard a loud shout from the throne, saying, 'Look, God's home is now among his people! He will live with them, and they will

---

13. *Book of Common Prayer*, 54.

Spiritual Tools

be his people. God himself will be with them. He will wipe every tear from their eyes, and there will be no more death or sorrow or crying or pain. All these things are gone forever.' And the one sitting on the throne said, 'Look, I am making everything new!'" (Rev 21:3–5).

Prayer of St. Ephraim:

"Lord and Master of my life, take from me the spirit of sloth, despondency, lust of power, and idle talk; but grant rather the spirit of chastity, humility, patience, and love to thy servant. Yea, O Lord and King, grant me to see my own transgressions, and not to judge my brother; for blessed art Thou unto the ages of ages. In the name of the Father and of the Son and of the Holy Spirit. Amen."[14]

12:00 P.M. (Sect)

"Give thanks to the Lord, for he is good! His faithful love endures forever. The Lord is my strength and my song; he has given me victory" (Ps 118:1, 14).

"For I know the plans I have for you, says the Lord. They are plans for good and not for disaster, to give you a future and a hope. In those days when you pray, I will listen. If you look for me wholeheartedly, you will find me" (Jer 29:11–13).

In the name of the Father and of the Son and of the Holy Spirit. Amen.

3:00 P.M. (None)

"For by grace are ye saved through faith; and that not of yourselves: it is the gift of God: Not of works, lest any man should boast. For we are his workmanship, created in Christ Jesus unto good works,

---

14. Mother Mary and Ware, *Lenten Triodion*, 69, 70; *Prayer Book for Orthodox Christians*, 9, 10.

which God hath before ordained that we should walk in them" (Eph 2:8–10).

"The Lord is king!
Let the earth rejoice!
Let the farthest coastlands be glad.
Dark clouds surround him.
Righteousness and justice are the foundation of his throne.
Fire spreads ahead of him
and burns up all his foes.
His lightning flashes out across the world.
The earth sees and trembles.
The mountains melt like wax before the Lord,
before the Lord of all the earth.
The heavens proclaim his righteousness;
every nation sees his glory.
For you, O Lord, are supreme over all the earth;
you are exalted far above all gods" (Ps 97).

"Be careful for nothing; but in everything by prayer and supplication with thanksgiving let your requests be made known unto God. And the peace of God, which passeth all understanding, shall keep your hearts and minds through Christ Jesus" (Phil 4:6, 7).

In the name of the Father and of the Son and of the Holy Spirit. Amen.

10:00 P.M. (COMPLINE)

"And rend your heart, and not your garments, and turn unto the Lord your God: for he is gracious and merciful, slow to anger, and of great kindness, and repenteth him of the evil" (Joel 2:13).

"For the message of the cross is foolishness to those who are perishing, but to us who are being saved it is the power of God" (1 Cor 1:18).

"Who may worship in your sanctuary, Lord?
Who may enter your presence on your holy hill?
Those who lead blameless lives and do what is right,
speaking the truth from sincere hearts.
Those who refuse to gossip
or harm their neighbors
or speak evil of their friends.
Those who despise flagrant sinners,
and honor the faithful followers of the Lord,
and keep their promises even when it hurts.
Those who lend money without charging interest,
and who cannot be bribed to lie about the innocent.
Such people will stand firm forever" (Ps 15).

As I lay down to sleep I remember the Gospel, that God was in Christ Jesus, reconciling the world to himself, not counting men's sins against them. God loves me, God has forgiven me, God is not mad at me, and God will never leave nor forsake me. Amen.

Monastic Hours—Prayer Discipline

The "monastic hours" are based on the typical practice found in most Christian monasteries. As stated above, these prayers are intended as a guide to help you develop your own prayer discipline and not as "rule" that must be followed. You need to determine your own "rule," what works for you.

O Lord, You have given me the gift of a new day. So work in me that what I do today might make a difference in my world. You delight in blessing me and making me more than a conqueror, so surround me, I pray, with your power and your favor. Let me never forget that you are the Lord of this world and I can do all things through Christ who strengthens me. Because of your great love for me and the power of your Holy Spirit, I will fear no enemy. May your name be lifted up and glorified in all the world, through Jesus Christ, our Lord. Amen

or
Lord Jesus, grant me
wisdom to live this day as if it were my last;
strength to do all that I must;
courage to do all that I should;
and humility to acknowledge that
I can do nothing without you.
In each moment, let me remember you;
praise and honor you;
contemplate your love and mercy;
and wonder at your loving kindness
to one who deserves it least.
Let me love as I am loved;
forgive as I am forgiven,
ever seeking to become like my savior.
Let me live this day eagerly
awaiting your return.
Come quickly, Lord Jesus. Amen.

Revival Prayer:
Gracious Father, we have taken you for granted,
We sit idle when we are meant to be on fire.
Revive us, Lord, empower us to seek your face,
To seek to be conformed to your image.
Rain down on us, we pray,
The power and presence of your Holy Spirit,
O Lord, revive Your Church!

Prayer for Enemies:
"Forgive those who hate us and do us wrong,
O Lord; do good unto them that do good unto us."[15]

---

15. *Prayer Book for Orthodox Christians*, 8, 9.

Spiritual Tools

Morning (Lauds)

In the Name of the Father, and of the Son, and of the Holy Spirit. Amen.

"Heavenly King, Comforter, the Spirit of truth, Who are everywhere present and fill all things, Treasury of every good and Giver of life; come and live in us, and cleanse us from every sin and save our souls, O Good One."[16]

"Holy God, Holy Mighty, Holy Immortal, have mercy on us." (Say three times.)[17]

"Glory to the Father, and to the Son, and to the Holy Spirit: as it was in the beginning, is now, and ever, and will be forever. Amen."[18]

If you live out what I taught you and make it part of your very existence, then you are truly my followers, those who seek to be just like me. Doing this, you will know what is true, and with that knowledge you will be free from all the influences of this world and be fit for service in the kingdom (paraphrase of John 8:31, 32).

"Most Holy Trinity, have mercy on us! Lord, cleanse us from our sins! Master, pardon our transgressions! Holy One, visit and heal our infirmities, for our Name's sake. Amen."[19]

"Submit yourselves therefore to God. Resist the devil, and he will flee from you. Draw near to God, and he will draw near to you. Cleanse your hands, you sinners, and purify your hearts, you double-minded. Humble yourselves before the Lord, and he will exalt you" (Jas 4: 7, 8, 10).

---

16. *Manual of Eastern Orthodox Prayers*, 2; *Prayerbook for Orthodox Christians*, 1.

17. Cherubim, *Manual of the Hours*, 3; *Prayerbook for Orthodox Christians*, 1.

18. *Book of Common Prayer*, 42.

19. Cherubim, *Manual of the Hours*, 3; *Manual for Eastern Orthodox Prayers*, 2.

The Disciple's Handbook

"Most merciful God, we confess that we have sinned against you in thought, word and deed, by what we have done, and by what we have left undone. We have not loved you with our whole heart; we have not loved our neighbors as ourselves. We are truly sorry and we humbly repent. For the sake of your Son Jesus Christ, have mercy on us and forgive us; that we may delight in your will, and walk in your ways to the glory of your Name. Amen."[20]

"Almighty God have mercy on us, forgive us all our sins through our Lord Jesus Christ, strengthen us in all goodness, and by the power of the Holy Spirit keep us in eternal life. Amen."[21]

Prayer of St. Polycarp of Smyrna:

I praise You for all things, I bless You, I glorify You through the eternal priest of heaven, Jesus Christ, Your beloved Son. Through Him be glory to You, together with Him and the Holy Spirit, now and forever. Amen.[22]

"But thanks be to God! He gives us the victory through the Lord Jesus Christ" (1 Cor 15:57).

"St. Michael the Archangel, defend us in battle; be our defense against the wickedness and snares of the devil. May God rebuke him we humbly pray. And do thou, O Prince of the Heavenly Host, by the power of God, cast into Hell Satan and all evil spirits, who wander the world seeking the ruin of souls. Amen."[23]

In the Name of the Father, and of the Son, and of the Holy Spirit. Amen.

---

20. *Book of Common Prayer*, 360.
21. *Book of Common Prayer*, 360.
22. Paraphrased from Lightfoot and Harmer, *The Apostolic Fathers*, 141.
23. Symonds, *Pope Leo XIII*, "Introduction."

Spiritual Tools

10:00 a.m. (Terce)

"Blessed be the God and Father of our Lord Jesus Christ, who has blessed us in Christ with every spiritual blessing in the heavenly places, even as he chose us in him before the foundation of the world, that we should be holy and blameless before him, in love" (Eph 1:3, 4).

"I believe in God the Father Almighty, Maker of heaven and earth; And in Jesus Christ his only Son, our Lord; who was conceived by the Holy Ghost, born of the Virgin Mary, suffered under Pontius Pilate, was crucified, dead, and buried; he descended into hell; the third day he rose again from the dead; he ascended into heaven, and sitteth on the right hand of God the Father Almighty; from thence he shall come to judge the quick and the dead. I believe in the Holy Ghost; the holy Catholic Church; the communion of the saints; the forgiveness of sins; the resurrection of the body; and the life everlasting. Amen."[24]

"I appeal to you therefore, brothers by the mercies of God, to present your bodies as a living sacrifice, holy and acceptable to God, which is your spiritual worship. Do not be conformed to this world but be transformed by the renewal of your mind, that by testing you may discern what is the will of God, what is good and acceptable and perfect" (Rom 12:1, 2).

Prayer of St. Ephraim:

"Lord and Master of my life, take from me the spirit of sloth, despondency, lust for power, and idle talk; But grant me rather the spirit of chastity, humility, patience, and love. Lord and King, grant me to see my own transgressions, and not to judge my brother; for you are blessed unto the ages of ages. Amen."[25]

---

24. *Book of Common Prayer*, 53, 54.
25. Mother Mary and Ware, *Lenten Triodion*, 69, 70.

"Do not be anxious about anything, but in everything by prayer and supplication with thanksgiving let your requests be made known to God. And the peace of God, which surpasses all understanding, will guard your hearts and your minds in Christ Jesus" (Phil 4:6–7).

"Hasten, O Father, the coming of thy kingdom, and grant that we, thy servants, who now live by faith, may with joy behold thy Son at His coming in glorious majesty, Jesus Christ, our only Mediator and Advocate. Amen."[26]

Prayer of St. Clement of Rome:

"Almighty God, Father of our Lord Jesus Christ, grant, we pray, that we might be grounded and settled in your truth by the coming of the Holy Spirit into our hearts. What we do not know, reveal to us; what is lacking within us, make complete; that which we do know, confirm in us; and keep us blameless in your service, through Jesus Christ our Lord."[27]

Prayer of St. Thomas Aquinas:

"Grant me, O Lord my God, a mind to know You, a heart to seek You, wisdom to find You, conduct pleasing to You, faithful perseverance in waiting for You, and a hope of finally embracing You."[28]

In the Name of the Father, and of the Son, and of the Holy Spirit. Amen.

---

26. *Book of Common Prayer*, 395.
27. Arnold, *Prayer of the Martyrs*, 30.
28. Thomas Aquinas, https://www.catholic.org/prayers/prayer.php?p=832.

12:00 p.m. (Sect)

In the Name of the Father, and of the Son, and of the Holy Spirit. Amen.

Grant, we pray, that we may draw closer to You in the life of the Spirit, that a holy desire may increase in us and that we may be sound of heart; and that we might stay immune from sin. We ask that there may be no wavering in our faith, no perversity in our minds, no slacking in our devotion, no relaxation in our pursuit of good works or in our love. Rather, may we be strong members of Your Holy Church. Amen.

Prayer of St. Columba:

"Alone with none but Thee, my God,
I journeyed on my way:
What need I fear, when Thou art near
O King of night and day?
More safe am I within Thy hand
than if a host did round me stand."[29]

"Live in peace with one another . . . be patient with all men. See that no one repays another with evil for evil, but always seek after that which is good for one another and for all men. Rejoice always; pray without ceasing; in everything give thanks; for this is God's will for you in Christ Jesus. Do not quench the Spirit; do not despise prophetic utterances. But examine everything carefully; hold fast to that which is good; abstain from every form of evil" (1 Thess 5:13b–22).

"Our Father, who art in heaven,
Hallowed be thy name,
Thy kingdom come,
Thy will be done,

---

29. St. Columba, http://poetryindex.blogspot.com/2009/08/alone-with-none-but-thee.html

On earth as it is in heaven.
Give us this day our daily bread, and forgive us our trespasses
As we forgive those who trespass against us,
And lead us not into temptation,
But deliver us from evil.
For thine is the kingdom and the power and the glory forever and
Ever, Amen."[30]

"For I know the plans I have for you, declares the Lord, plans for welfare and not for evil, to give you a future and a hope. Then you will call upon me and come and pray to me, and I will hear you. You will seek me and find me, when you seek me with all your heart" (Jer 29:11–13).

In the name of the Father and of the Son and of the Holy Spirit. Amen.

3:00 p.m. (None)

"For by grace are ye saved through faith; and that not of yourselves: it is the gift of God: Not of works, lest any man should boast. For we are his workmanship, created in Christ Jesus unto good works, which God hath before ordained that we should walk in them" (Eph 2:8–10).

"For You are the Resurrection, the Life, and the Repose of Your servants who have fallen asleep, Lord Christ our God, unto You we ascribe glory, together with the Father, who is from everlasting, and Your all-holy, good, and life-creating Spirit, now and ever unto ages of ages. Amen."[31]

"He saved us, not because of works done by us in righteousness, but according to his own mercy, by the washing of regeneration

---

30. *Book of Common Prayer*, 54

31. "Akathist for the Repose of Those Who Have Fallen Asleep," http://www.orthodox.net/akathists/akathist-for-those-who-have-fallen-asleep.pdf, 18.

and renewal of the Holy Spirit, whom he poured out on us richly through Jesus Christ our Savior" (Titus 3: 5, 6).

Prayer of St. Benedict:

"Bestow upon me, O Gracious, O Holy Father:
Intellect to understand you,
Perceptions to perceive you purely,
Reason to discern you,
Wisdom to find you,
A spirit to know you.
A heart to meditate upon you,
Ears to hear you,
Eyes to behold you,
A tongue to proclaim you,
A conversation pleasing to you,
Patience to wait for you,
A perseverance to look for you.
Grant me a perfect end—your holy Presence.
Grant me a blessed resurrection, and your recompense, everlasting life. Amen."[32]

"For we do not have a high priest who is unable to sympathize with our weaknesses, but one who in every respect has been tempted as we are, yet without sin. Let us then with confidence draw near to the throne of grace, that we may receive mercy and find grace to help in time of need" (Heb 4:15–16).

Revival Prayer:

Gracious Father, we have taken you for granted,
We sit idle when we are meant to be on fire.
Revive us, Lord, empower us to seek your face,
To seek to be conformed to your image.

---

32. St. Benedict, https://blessedsacramentwalpole.org/treasury-of-catholic-prayers

Rain down on us, we pray,
The power and presence of your Holy Spirit,
O Lord, revive your church!

Lord, keep my lips from speaking evil of my fellow man. Give me grace and favor that I might bless instead of curse; praise instead of criticize; encourage instead of put down.

"He has shown you, O man, what is good. And what does the Lord require of you? To act justly and to love mercy and to walk humbly with your God" (Mic 6:8).

In the Name of the Father, and of the Son, and of the Holy Spirit. Amen.

6:00 p.m. (Vespers)

In the Name of the Father, and of the Son, and of the Holy Spirit. Amen.

"Heavenly King, Comforter, the Spirit of truth, Who are everywhere present and fill all things, Treasury of every good and Giver of life; come and live in us, and cleanse us from every sin and save our souls, O Good One."[33]

"Holy God, Holy Mighty, Holy Immortal, have mercy on us." (Say three times.)[34]

"Glory to the Father, and to the Son, and to the Holy Spirit: as it was in the beginning, is now, and ever, and will be forever. Amen."[35]

"If you abide in my word, you are truly my disciples, and you will know the truth, and the truth will set you free" (John 8:31, 32).

---

33. Cherubim, *Manual of the Hours*, 2.
34. Cherubim, *Manual of the Hours*, 3.
35. *Book of Common Prayer*, 42.

Spiritual Tools

"Most Holy Trinity, have mercy on us! Lord, cleanse us from our sins! Master, pardon our transgressions! Holy One, visit and heal our infirmities, for thy Name's sake. Amen."[36]

"Submit yourselves therefore to God. Resist the devil, and he will flee from you. Draw near to God, and he will draw near to you. Cleanse your hands, you sinners, and purify your hearts, you double-minded. Humble yourselves before the Lord, and he will exalt you" (Jas 4:7, 8, 10).

"Most merciful God, we confess that we have sinned against you in thought, word and deed, by what we have done, and by what we have left undone. We have not loved you with our whole heart; we have not loved our neighbors as ourselves. We are truly sorry and we humbly repent. For the sake of your Son Jesus Christ, have mercy on us and forgive us; that we may delight in your will, and walk in your ways to the glory of your Name. Amen."[37]

"Almighty God have mercy on us, forgive us all our sins through our Lord Jesus Christ, strengthen us in all goodness, and by the power of the Holy Spirit keep us in eternal life. Amen."[38]

"The reason the Son of God appeared was to destroy the works of the devil" (1 John 3:8b).

"For though we walk in the flesh, we are not waging war according to the flesh. For the weapons of our warfare are not of the flesh but have divine power to destroy strongholds. We destroy arguments and every lofty opinion raised against the knowledge of God, and take every thought captive to obey Christ" (2 Cor 10:3–7).

"Let not your hearts be troubled. Believe in God; believe also in me . . . I am the way, and the truth, and the life. No one comes to the Father except through me" (John 14:1, 6).

---

36. Cherubim, *Manual of the Hours*, 3.
37. *Book of Common Prayer*, 360.
38. *Book of Common Prayer*, 360.

"But the fruit of the Spirit is love, joy, peace, patience, kindness, goodness, faithfulness, gentleness and self-control" (Gal 5:22, 23a).

"St. Michael the Archangel, defend us in battle; be our defense against the wickedness and snares of the devil. May God rebuke him we humbly pray. And do thou, O Prince of the Heavenly Host, by the power of God, cast into Hell Satan and all evil spirits, who wander the world seeking the ruin of souls. Amen."[39]

In the Name of the Father, and of the Son, and of the Holy Spirit. Amen.

10:00 p.m. (Compline)

In the Name of the Father, and of the Son, and of the Holy Spirit. Amen.

O God of love and giver of oneness of heart, who granted unto us, through your only begotten Son, the new commandment that we love one another as you have loved us the unworthy and sinful; we ask you, our Lord, grant us your servants, throughout our lifetime on earth, thoughts that do not recall to memory former evil deeds and a conscience without hypocrisy, but grant us faithful thoughts and a heart full of brotherly love.[40]

"Glory to the Father, and to the Son, and to the Holy Spirit: as it was in the beginning, is now, and ever, and will be forever. Amen."[41]

Prayer of Julian of Norwich:

"God, of your goodness, give me yourself; for you are sufficient for me. I cannot properly ask anything less, to be worthy of you.

---

39. Symonds, *Pope Leo XIII*, "Introduction."

40. Adapted from the Liturgy of St. Cyril, http://www.copticchurch.net/topics/liturgy/liturgy_of_st_cyril.pdf.

41. *Book of Common Prayer*, 4.

Spiritual Tools

If I were to ask less, I should always be in want. In you alone do I have all."[42]

"Trust in the Lord with all your heart and lean not on your own understanding; in all your ways acknowledge him, and he will make your paths straight. Do not be wise in your own eyes; fear the Lord and shun evil. This will bring health to your body and nourishment to your bones" (Prov 3:5–8).

"Rejoice in the Lord always; again I will say, rejoice. Let your reasonableness be known to everyone. The Lord is at hand; do not be anxious about anything, but in everything by prayer and supplication with thanksgiving let your requests be made known to God. And the peace of God, which surpasses all understanding, will guard your hearts and your minds in Christ Jesus" (Phil 4:4–7).

"And they have conquered him by the blood of the Lamb and by the word of their testimony, for they loved not their lives even unto death. Therefore, rejoice, O heavens and you who dwell in them! But woe to you, O earth and sea, for the devil has come down to you in great wrath, because he knows that his time is short!" (Rev 12:11, 12).

"St. Michael the Archangel, defend us in battle; be our defense against the wickedness and snares of the devil. May God rebuke him we humbly pray. And do thou, O Prince of the Heavenly Host, by the power of God, cast into Hell Satan and all evil spirits, who wander the world seeking the ruin of souls. Amen."[43]

In the Name of the Father, and of the Son, and of the Holy Spirit. Amen.

---

42. From Belief Net, https://www.beliefnet.com/prayers/christian/comfort/i-have-all-in-god.aspx.

43. Symonds, *Pope Leo XIII*, "Introduction."

Celebration Lifestyle

Dallas Willard calls celebration "one of the most important disciplines."[44] This is the point where our lives and God meet. In Christian circles this is called "worship" and "fellowship." In the '70s it was also called "*koinonia*." The purpose of this time of celebration was to praise God, rejoice in his kingdom, and in his blessings. In Deuteronomy 14:22–27 the Israelites were to bring in the tithe or one tenth of all they had received from the harvest in order to have a tremendous party. This was a time to rejoice with the community of faith and remember God's goodness that year. Paul also tells us, "Rejoice in the Lord always. I will say it again: Rejoice!" (Phil 4:4). We serve God who calls on us to celebrate his blessings and party in his honor.

Our life in Christ is to be filled with the "abundance" of his kingdom. Christianity has too often been associated with the idea that life is so serious that somehow to have a good time is sinful. Quite the opposite is true. God commands us to rejoice and enjoy him. That is why the Westminster Catechism begins with this question, "What is the chief end of man?" and answers it, "The chief end of man is to love God and enjoy him forever."[45] We are called to a life of joy and celebration in the presence of the King of kings.

That does not mean there won't be times of sorrow and times of weeping; there will be. But joy is so much more than laughter or the absence of pain. We have so many reasons for joy. One reason is the wonderful irony that we see in the world God has created. So much of our worldview is often based on the lies we are told by the world and the devil. Joy is a worldview based on the truth, the world as it is and not merely how we see it. God paid the price for our sin on the cross through the sacrifice of Jesus. But he did more than that. Our Lord came to defeat the devil and all of his works and to set us about the task of mopping up after Satan's defeat (1 John 3:8b). If we will look at the world in this light, we see that our

---

44. Willard, *The Spirit of the Disciplines*, 86.
45. *Westminster Catechism*, Question 1; Chan, *Liturgical Theology*, 55.

way, during either good or bad times, is part of a greater movement whose end is utterly glorious.

Worship

What is Worship?

Worship is, on the one hand, a natural reaction to our relationship with God. It is engaged in within the community of faith as well as in the daily life of individual believers. On the other hand, it is also something subject to our will in that it requires definite action. This makes it, in some ways, dependent on a variety of motivations and circumstances. Even so, it is always done in reference to the community of faith. Even individual worship, done outside or apart from corporate gatherings, is part of the collective action of that community. Private prayers, for example, involve the participation and direction of the Holy Spirit (Rom 8:26), as do all devotional activities. This must, therefore, be part of the worship of the whole. All worship is corporate because it comes from the same Spirit and is directed through the one kingdom to Christ at the altar in heaven. There is, in a very real sense, no such thing in Christianity as individual or private religion.

Liturgy (the work of the church) is the first form of Christian discipleship training which leads us into the culture and mindset of the church. In the liturgy, the world ceases to rotate around "me" and centers on God.[46] Whether you come from a "low" or "high" church background, you have a form of liturgy, a pattern of worship that you follow. This has been true from the very beginning of the church (1 Cor 11:23–32).

Some people say they can worship anywhere or that they can function as a Christian outside the fellowship of the church. In one sense this is true, but in a very real way it's not. When a person is in worship, that person is part of the functioning of the whole of the church, but is missing out on the encouragement, fellowship, and discipline to be found there. It is possible to live as a Christian

---

46. Chan, *Liturgical Theology*, 43.

without these things but difficult to grow and mature in their absence. It would be easier to grow a flower in concrete than to reach Christian maturity outside the church.

There is also the potential for serious problems in the life of the believer if the corporate part of worship is ignored. First, a "Lone Ranger" style of Christianity leaves one open to theological error. There is a tendency to believe that your way of doing things is the only right way to do them. The Eastern Orthodox Church has always taught that theology (knowledge and experience of God) is passed on through what we do in corporate worship. Elements of worship such as the creed, hymns, the Lord's Prayer, and the Eucharist (Lord's Supper) are critical for maintaining theological orthodoxy.[47]

Second, we are commanded in Hebrews 10:25: "Not forsaking the assembling of ourselves together." This is a continuation of the teaching and practice of the Old Testament where certain times were set aside, including the Sabbath, to gather as God's people for worship (Lev 8:4; Num 10:3). Being a disciple of Jesus Christ means more than individual salvation (John 3:16). It also means being a part of the kingdom of God. When one is part of a kingdom one benefits from the blessings of the king. One receives the prayers, encouragement, and support of others in the kingdom. Most importantly, however, one participates in the special presence of our Lord and King within the corporate actions of his gathered people. This is true not only for the Eucharist (Lord's Supper) but for every action in the liturgy (the work of the people) as it is directed toward God.

Both individual and corporate actions are necessary in the life of the disciple. To be a disciple means to personally follow a master. The master in this case is the King of kings and Lord of Lords, which makes that disciple part of a greater whole to which he/she has responsibilities. We were created to have a relationship with our Lord. Since he is who he is and has done what he has

---

47. Ware, *The Orthodox Church*; Justin Martyr, *First Apology*, ch.64–68, https://d2y1pz2y630308.cloudfront.net/15471/documents/2016/10/St.%20Justin%20Martyr-The%20First%20Apology%20of%20Justin.pdf.

done, we owe him all our love and our worship. He has called us to walk humbly with him and to gather together for worship. We must neglect neither.

As we worship, things happen in the spiritual realm. The presence of the Lord is within us in all that we do and all of our life in worship. The enemy does not want us in touch with the power of the Holy Spirit in our lives which is available to us in worship. Worship does not end as we leave the church. We walk out into the world as an heir of Christ and a priest/king of the Most High.

We must also understand that the knowledge of God's will lives in the church, which is supremely the hearer and bearer of the word. Therefore, individual Christians come to know God's will primarily within the living relationship with his community.

Forms of Worship

In the first apology of Justin Martyr, beginning in chapter 64, we are told about how Christians worshiped in the middle of the second century CE. Most Christians reading these words will recognize their own worship experience. Justin is describing what had been the common practice of the church for some time. This form of worship has clear ties to the worship of the synagogue and also elements that go back to Jewish temple rituals.[48] We see synagogue worship in the basic form of the service including the reading and exposition of the Bible. The temple is clearly present in both the vestments of the clergy and in the sacrifice of the Eucharist (Lord's Supper).

This does not mean that worship must be restricted to these forms, but it does tell us that God has a basic form of worship that he desires his people to follow (Ex 28:2–18; 40–41; Lev 1–7). Yet, within these forms, there is an almost endless opportunity for variation and creativity. It was true even from the beginnings of the church that each community, while adhering to the general forms of worship above, had its own individual variations. There

---

48. Pelikan, *Emergence of the Catholic Tradition*, 26.

needs to be a liturgy (the work of the people), but within this form we are free to use the creativity he has given us to express our love for him through his gifts.[49]

This is, of course, where things can get tricky. Many Christians love the way that they worship, and that's great. On the other hand, some also believe that their way of worship is the only way that God approves. Others are so caught up in their form of worship that any suggestion of change is taken as a threat to good order in the church. Christians can get very upset over these issues. It is not the purpose of this book to tell you *how* you ought to worship, but merely *that* you ought to worship. The point is not to direct you to any specific form of worship besides that mentioned above in Justin's work, which seems to be the basic form in most churches anyway. Rather, there are only a few suggestions I would offer on forms of worship.

First, worship should glorify God the Father, God the Son, and God the Holy Spirit. Second, it should be rooted in the Scriptures and the creeds. Third, it should reflect the genuine mind, ethos, and feelings of the community of faith you belong to. Last, as the community of faith grows and matures, it should be open to the leading of the Spirit to change to reflect that growth. This should be the work of the Spirit as clearly experienced by the whole community and never done simply to do something different. Traditions are good but need to be flexible and at the disposal of the Holy Spirit. Traditions that are not able to function dynamically through the moving of the Holy Spirit are harmful to the growth of the church.

Fellowship

The idea of "fellowship" is where some real reeducation needs to take place in the church. We tend to place fellowship as one of the incidentals of the church with the same spiritual significance as the color of the carpeting or the type of flora in the front of the church

---

49. Webber, *Ancient-Future Time*, 152.

building. Christian fellowship, and especially the meals associated with it, are critical elements within the life of the church.

In the covenant of the Old Testament, one of the most significant activities of worship was the covenant meal (Lev 2–7). There were only a few sacrifices performed to cover sin (Lev 1:1; 4:3; 5:6). The vast majority of the sacrificial system was designed to promote intimacy with God (Lev 2:1). One of the most effective tools for the development of that intimacy was the sacred meal. You would call your friends and family together to feast before the Lord, to celebrate with a sacred meal (Lev 7:11–16).

The biblical admonition on the nature of this relationship is found in 1 John: "If someone says, 'I love God,' and hates his brother, he is a liar; for the one who does not love his brother whom he has seen, cannot love God whom he has not seen" (1 John 4:20). This is the intent of the sacred meals in Leviticus. As you ate with your family and friends, you developed intimacy with them. In doing so, you were also developing intimacy with God since he is present in each of them and when you love them, you love him (Gen 1:26, 27; Matt 24:40; John 1:9). This concept becomes even more important when applied to those in the church, especially those that are difficult to love. Christ is in those people too and even in those outside the church.

Contemplation

There are many wonderful works written, especially in the Roman Catholic and Eastern Orthodox traditions, on this subject, and I will not attempt to compete with them. The practice of lectio divina and the use of the prayer rope are the closest that I have come to contemplative activity, so it is these that I have included here.

Lectio Divina

Lectio divina is a monastic practice of total immersion of the reader into the word of God. It is not primarily an intellectual but a spiritual exercise. The intent of the practice is to saturate us with the Bible and help shape the whole of our inner person and outward activity. Ruminating on the word (chewing it over in our mind and heart) is essential to this exercise. Through it we absorb the text into our very being. The goal of this practice is spiritual transformation through experiencing God in the Scripture. It should be noted that this is in no way a "magical" activity. By following this practice one cannot achieve a predictable result. Lectio divina is based on the understanding that the Bible as the Word of God is first and primarily a person and not a book. Jesus is the Word of God and is made accessible to us through the enlightenment of the Holy Spirit in the very words of the text of Scripture.[50]

To begin, take time to ready your spirit through prayer and stillness. Begin your reading in the Scriptures at the last place you left off. (This can become a continuous process as a part of your regular devotions.) Read very slowly with your mind and heart open. Don't study the text, just read it slowly. Although it is not necessary to read it aloud, I have found that it helps me focus on the words as I hear them.

When a word or phrase makes an impression on your mind and heart, stop reading. Begin the *Meditatio*: the absorption of the word through repetition. Meditate with this Scripture by repeating it again and again within your heart or aloud. Don't try to find meaning or interpret the word at this point, just experience it. This repetition allows you to savor the words. After a while you may become aware of an impression that the words have made. It is time to begin the *Oratio*: your prayerful response.

Express to God the impression his word has made on you. Keep it simple and pray spontaneously. Your prayer may move into *Contemplatio*: a simple being-in-Christ with God. No one knows how God will use this time with him in the word to speak to you (you can't "cue" the Holy Spirit) but you may be sure that he will meet you in the intimacy of your interaction with his Word.[51]

---

50. Manss and Frohlich, *The Lay Contemplative*, 54.
51. Pennington, *Lectio Divina*, 88–90.

Spiritual Tools

Meditation and contemplation, as used in monastic prayer, is sometimes a difficult discipline for Christians outside of Roman Catholic or Orthodox communions to use, mainly because we are not used to it or have little experience with this form of spirituality. There is also a tendency to equate what is done in eastern non-Christian traditions with these Christian practices and experiences. An article in *The Lay Contemplative* suggests that "to help make sense of the diversity of experience in contemplation, we need to recognize the basic principle that, . . . human beings are created with a contemplative core. We were created to love God, to know God, to be in union with God. Our truest and most original being lives in deepest intimacy with God."[52] Therefore, since "we always are, always have been and always will be in God's presence . . . contemplative experience is potentially available to every human being at all times and in every circumstance."[53]

Having said that, it is important to note that many who write about Christian contemplation provide little help in their attempt to describe what goes on in this process. It is only certain that for each person the experience will be, in some way, unique. This should, however, come as no surprise since contemplation is, in essence, an intimate communion with God. As such, it must be unique since the relationship between the parties involved is unique. If we cannot describe the precise nature of what is likely to be experienced in Christian contemplation, we can describe some of the methods that have been employed in its pursuit.

The commentary on the Rule of Benedict (RB 1980) states that "Benedict's knowledge of the tradition (meditative or contemplative prayer) is profound . . . through assimilation . . . of truth that comes from long application to lectio divina" as described above.[54] The lectio divina is "listening to a person present. God lives in his Word. The Word is a Divine Presence."[55]

---

52. Manss and Frohlich, *The Lay Contemplative*, 54.
53. Fry, *Rule of St. Benedict*, 178.
54. Fry, *Rule of St. Benedict*, 178.
55. Pennington, *Lectio Divina*, 4.

In the practical working of the monastery, the purpose of the lectio divina was to keep the monks saturated with the word of God. In RB 1980 it says, "About four hours each day was devoted to the lectio, which included reading, private prayer and the meditatio (memorization, repetition, and rumination on biblical texts). This prayerful reflection upon Scripture and its interpretation by the Fathers and monastic writers kept the monk's mind constantly filled with the word of God and helped to shape the whole of his inner psychology and outward activity."[56] This idea of "rumination" continued into the practice of meditation. This was a method of infusing the text into the mind. "For the ancients, the term meditation meant something different from what it does for us today. It was not a purely interior activity but involved the repetition of a text aloud . . . it meant that the reader repeated passages over and over again in order to learn them by heart. Once learned, these texts could then be repeated from memory without a book."[57]

As a part of a summer grant, I had a chance to witness this type of monastic meditation in a pilgrimage to the Abbey of Gethsemane outside Louisville, KY. It the first "hour" of the day (3:15 a.m.) the monks chanted selected psalms by heart in the almost total darkness of the chapel. In their sister-house, the Monastery of the Holy Spirit in Conyers, GA, the monks also keep a thirty-minute silence after the chanting of the Psalms. They sit in the Nave with the laity so that, in the profound quiet, the reality of God's word has the opportunity to infuse the worshiper with Christ's presence.

This process was also used for private prayer, especially of those new to the cloister. "He [the novice] may also have memorized passages that were to be chewed over or ruminated upon later as a stimulus to private prayer . . . it was a common practice."[58] The purpose of this practice was spiritual transformation. "The novice's meditatio, then, was a kind of study, but not in the modern sense;

---

56. Manss and Frohlich, *The Lay Contemplative*, 54.
57. Fry, *Rule of St. Benedict*, 95.
58. Fry, *Rule of St. Benedict*, 95.

Spiritual Tools

it was confined to sacred texts, principally Scripture, and its goal was not purely intellectual, but an existential appropriation of the Word in view of forming his life. It was an activity as closely related to prayer as to study; medieval monastic writers considered lectio, meditatio, oratio and contemplatio to be four successive phases of a single movement involving the mind, the heart, the will and the body."[59]

Contemplation is the active engagement of the whole being in the word of God. It brings a person into the very presence of God "that it might help us to develop the practice or habit of spending some time each day intimately with the Lord."[60] The change brought on by the application of this discipline is entirely from the Holy Spirit. It is not something that can be induced from the mere practice of contemplation. In it one is not attempting to somehow gain merit from God by one's piety but rather to come into the presence of God with the whole of one's being.[61]

On the more practical side, there are as many ideas on how the lectio divina should be employed as there are writers on the subject. The methodology suggested below is just one of many and has been simplified for the beginner. This is not as much a form of prayer as a method of meeting God in the word. The practice is more that of listening than of trying to understand with the mind. We must come to this discipline with the intention to hear the voice of God with our heart and soul.

This idea has been expressed by Bishop Kallistos Ware, "There are no fixed and unvarying rules, necessarily imposed on all who seek to pray; and equally, there is no mechanical technique, whether physical or mental, which can compel God to manifest his presence. His grace is conferred always as a free gift, and cannot be gained automatically by any method or technique. The encounter between Good and man in the kingdom of the heart is therefore marked by an inexhaustible variety of patterns."[62] Pennington

---

59. Fry, *Rule of St. Benedict*, 446.
60. Pennington, *Lectio Divina*, xii–xiii.
61. Fry, *Rule of St. Benedict*, 179; Casey, *The Benedictine Handbook*, 106–9.
62. Ware, *The Power of the Name*, 3.

says, "We believe not only that the Word who is God speaks to us through the inspired Word, but that the Word is truly present in his inspired Word and present to us as he communicates with us through the Word."[63]

A Simple Form of Lectio Divina

- Location: Find a quiet place where you won't be disturbed to begin the lectio divina.
- Prayer: Begin with a simple prayer to prepare your heart for the lessons that God has for you during this time with him.
- Lectio: The reading; slowly begin reading aloud from the Scripture (lectionary, daily office, regular reading of a book of the Bible). This is not a time to study, so do not let your intellect dwell on the words. When a particular passage, phrase, or even a single word moves you, stop reading and write down the passage, phrase, or word to remember it.
- Meditatio: Repeat aloud the passage, word, or phrase, slowly over and over, either verbally or silently within your mind and heart. Savor the words; don't try to figure them out. The purpose of this time of meditation is to be open to what God wants to say to you through his word. This is the listening time.
- Oratio: Respond to what God is revealing to you by prayer. Tell God the impression the word has made on you. Ask the questions it has provoked in you.
- Contemplatio: This is a simple time of intimacy with God. You may be aware of being drawn closer to God. Let this inner communication through his word shape your thinking. As you ruminate or chew over the word, let it infuse itself into your mind, soul, and heart.[64]

---

63. Pennington, *Lectio Divina*, xii.
64. Fry, *Rule of St. Benedict*, 177.

Spiritual Tools

The Jesus Prayer—Orthodox Spirituality

A similar technique is used in the Orthodox tradition and is referred to as "the Jesus Prayer." The Jesus Prayer itself reads: "Lord Jesus Christ, Son of God, have mercy upon me, a sinner." First of all, the Jesus Prayer is centered on the name of Jesus because this is the name of him whom "God has highly exalted," the name given to the Lord by God himself (Luke 1:31), the "name which is above every name" (Phil 2:9–10; Eph 1:21), "for there is no other name given among men by which we must be saved" (Acts 4:12). All prayer for Christians must be performed in the name of Jesus: "if you ask anything in my name, I will do it" (John 14:13–14). That Jesus is the Christ, and that the Christ is Lord, is the essence of the Christian faith and the foundation of the Christian church. To believe and proclaim this is granted by the Holy Spirit: "no one can say 'Jesus is Lord' except by the Holy Spirit" (1 Cor 12:3), and "every tongue shall confess that Jesus Christ is Lord to the glory of God the Father" (Phil 2:11).

Calling Jesus "Son of God" is to acknowledge God as his Father. To do this is, at the same time, to have God as one's own Father, and this too is granted by the indwelling Spirit. "And when the time had fully come, God sent forth His Son, born of a woman, born under the law, to redeem those who were under the law, so that we might receive adoption as sons. And because you are sons, God has sent the Spirit of His Son into our hearts, crying 'Abba! Father!'" (Gal 4:4-6). When we cry "Abba! Father!" it is the Spirit himself bearing witness with our spirit that we are children of God (Rom 8:15–16). Thus, to pray "Lord Jesus Christ, Son of God" is already to be a child of God and to be certain that the Holy Spirit is in you.

In this way, the Jesus Prayer brings the Spirit of God into the heart of man. "Have mercy on me a sinner" is the publican's prayer. When uttered with humble conviction, it brings divine justification (Luke 18:13). Generally speaking, divine mercy is what man needs most of all. It is for this reason that the numberless repetition of requests for the Lord's mercy is found everywhere in the prayers of the church. And finally, all men are sinners. To know this is a fact, and to confess it with faith, is to be justified and forgiven by God (Rom 3:10–12; Ps 14:1–3).

The Jesus Prayer is a method for unceasing prayer (1 Thess 5:16). The Eastern Orthodox practice is as follows: repeat the prayer constantly and continually, whatever one is doing, without any particular bodily postures or breathing techniques. This is the way taught by St. Gregory Palamas in his short discourse about how unceasing mental prayer is the duty of all Christians.[65] Anyone can do this, whatever his occupation or position in life. This is also shown in the Orthodox classic *The Way of a Pilgrim*. The purpose and results of this method of prayer are those generally of all prayer: that one might be continually united with God by unceasing remembrance of his presence and the perpetual invocation of his name, so that one might always serve him and all men with the virtues of Christ and the fruits of the Spirit.[66] But it must be remembered that although this is a routine and repetitive act of prayer, "the name of Jesus is not a talisman or 'magic formula,' . . . and 'the Jesus prayer is not a technique but an act of love. It expresses a direct relationship between persons.'"[67]

The Jesus Prayer is also a tool for defense against the insinuations of the devil. You should have it ready for times of temptation. The practice of the Jesus prayer "consists in acquiring the habit of keeping the intellect on guard within the heart."[68] In this way, as St. John Climacus has said, "you can 'flog your enemies,' i.e. the temptations, with the name of Jesus for there is no stronger weapon in heaven or on earth."[69] This method works best when one practices the prayer without ceasing, joining "to every breath a sober invocation of Jesus' name." When one practices the continual

---

65. Meyendorff, *St. Gregory Palamas*, 17.
66. Bacovcin, *Way of a Pilgrim*, 17.
67. Gillet, *The Jesus Prayer*, 15.
68. Gillet, *The Jesus Prayer*, 79.
69. Palmer et al., *The Philokalia*, 42.

"prayer of the heart," and when the temptations to sin enter the heart, they are met by the prayer and are defeated by grace.[70]

Prayer Rope Prayers

The use of the prayer rope or "rosary" goes back to early monastic times. It was first used by the monks to keep track of the 150 Psalms that were recited by them, in many cases, weekly. In later years, laymen took up using it but substituted the Lord's Prayer for the Psalms. In more recent times the "Hail Mary" prayer with prayers remembering the suffering and triumph of Jesus became the norm in the Roman Catholic Church. Following the Eastern Orthodox tradition, I suggest using the Jesus Prayer as the main prayer of this discipline. These prayers, as indicated below, are set up for the "Anglican Rosary" of ten decades. (A decade is ten beads or knots separated by larger beads or knots.) These prayers can also be adapted for use with an Orthodox prayer rope of thirty-three, one hundred, or three hundred knots.[71]

Traditional Prayer Rope

Cross: In the Name of the Father, and of the Son, and of the Holy Spirit. Amen.

Small Knot: Glory to you, O God, Glory to you.

Joining Large Knot: O Heavenly King, Comforter, Spirit of Truth, Who are in all places and fill all things; Treasury of blessings and Giver of life: Come and dwell in me, and cleanse me from every stain, and save my soul, O Good One. Amen.

Spaces after Large Knot: Glory to the Father, and to the Son, and to the Holy Spirit, as it was in the beginning, is now, and will be forever. Amen.

---

70. Meyendorff, *St. Gregory Palamas*, 130.
71. Fry, *Rule of St. Benedict*, 180.

Small Knots: Lord Jesus Christ, Son of God, have mercy upon me, a sinner.

Second Large Knot: Holy God, Holy and Mighty, Holy Immortal One, have mercy on us. (3X)

Third Large Knot: O Most Holy Trinity, have mercy on me. Lord, cleanse me from my sins. Master, pardon my iniquities. Holy God, visit me and heal my infirmities for the glory of your Name.

Fourth Large Knot: Holy God, Holy and Mighty, Holy Immortal One, have mercy on us. (3X)

Joining Large Knot: Our Father, who art in heaven, hallowed be thy Name; thy kingdom come; thy will be done on earth, as it is in heaven. Give us this day our daily bread; and forgive us our trespasses, as we forgive those who trespass against us; and lead us not into temptation, but deliver us from evil.

Small Knot by Cross: The Father is my hope; the Son is my refuge; the Holy Spirit is my protector. All-holy Trinity, glory to you. Amen.

Cross: In the Name of the Father, and of the Son, and of the Holy Spirit. Amen.[72]

Orthodox Thirty-Three-Knot Prayer Rope

Cross: In the Name of the Father, and of the Son, and of the Holy Spirit. Glory to you, Lord Christ; Glory to you! Holy God, Holy Mighty, Holy Immortal, Have mercy on us. ("Holy God . . ." 3X)

Knots: Lord Jesus Christ, Son of God, have mercy upon me, a sinner.

Middle Divider: Heavenly King, Comforter, Spirit of Truth, come and dwell in me so I might become like my savior. Amen. Glory to

---

72. Adapted from *The Customary of the Society of St. Seraphim*, 5.

Spiritual Tools

the Father, and to the Son, and to the Holy Spirit, as it was in the beginning, is now, and will be forever. Amen.

After Complete Circle: Our Father, who art in heaven, Hallowed be thy name, thy kingdom come, thy will be done, on earth as it is in heaven. Give us this day our daily bread, and forgive us our trespasses as we forgive those who trespass against us, and lead us not into temptation, but deliver us from evil. For thine is the kingdom and the power and the glory forever and ever. Amen.

Cross: In the Name of the Father, and of the Son, and of the Holy Spirit. Amen.[73]

The Ebenezer Stone

This form of contemplation and encouragement is based on the practice of setting up memorials in Israel after significant events in order to remember them.[74] In 1 Samuel 7:12, the prophet Samuel sets up a stone to commemorate Israel's victory over the Philistines and calls it "Ebenezer" or "stone of help."[75] Like Israel, we use a stone as a physical reminder that God has been our help and provision in the past and, therefore, we can trust him to be so in our future. It is a tool to remind us of his faithfulness. We use a semi-precious amethyst because it is the traditional stone used in the bishop's ring but any stone will do just as well. When we see and handle it, it is a physical reminder of what God has done and is doing in our lives. This is just another way to keep God in our minds each day.

---

73. See "Using a Prayer Rope," https://www.orthodoxprayer.org/Prayer%20Rope.html.
74. Bratcher, Marc, Z. "Memorials," HBD 625.
75. Way, R. J. "Ebenezer," NBD 294–95.

Contemplation in the Digital Age

We are rapidly developing media habits that seriously interfere with spiritual growth. Spiritual comfort, guidance, and intimacy do not come from a machine. Entertainment and the like are fine, but we still need time apart, time to listen, pray, and meditate. In short, we need time in our own heads to think, feel, and process all the data that is being thrown at us on a daily basis. Socrates said, "The unexamined life is not worth living," and I think he was right.[76] We don't need to throw away our digital tools, but perhaps remind ourselves that they are tools, something to help us live our lives rather than the reason for it. They can be a great help to our spiritual growth if used properly. My daily organization, Bible reading and research, journaling, and praying discipline are all done using digital tools. But I also need time off from them to mull over the things I am learning. Use the tools as tools but do not be controlled by them.

Solitude and Silence

Example of Jesus' Life

Jesus is our great example of prayer in the Bible. There are many of his prayers recorded in the Gospels, yet there are many that are only hinted at. These are the prayers that he did not share with his disciples when he went off alone to pray (Matt 4:8; 14:23; Mark 1:35; 6:46; Luke 4:5; 5:16; 6:12; 9:28). One of Jesus' most poignant prayers that we have, during his intense suffering in the garden of Gethsemane, was at a time when he was alone since the disciples had fallen asleep (Matt 26:36–46; Mark 14:32–42; Luke 22:39–46). We don't know for sure why Jesus felt the need to be alone with God for prayer other than the reasons we have in our own lives. We all need times of solitude and silence, both to get our emotional equilibrium back and to spend time with God. We do know

---

76. Plato, *Apology*, 38a5–6.

Spiritual Tools

that Jesus took time to be alone and seemed to need that time with God.

Methods of Solitude

There are about as many ways as there are people of getting into a state, mindset, or physical locality where we can be alone with God. The old prayer closet is still a great idea. The most important feature though is the practical one. Go someplace that is quiet, set apart, and free from distractions where you can pray without interruption. In our very busy world this can often be a difficult task. One method that works well even in the busiest situations is to imagine yourself in a comfortable chair, in a well-lit room, surrounded by hardwood paneling, with soft music playing. In this room inside yourself, you can shut out distractions in all but the most difficult of circumstances. Doing this helps focus one's attention on praying. This is not a prescription on how to find solitude in the hustle and bustle of a busy world, just one example of how it can be done.

In the Orthodox tradition, the person seeking silence was a type of monk called a "Hesychast."[77] Their idea of solitude is best illustrated by the following quotation. "Silence is not merely negative . . . [it is] an attitude of attentive alertness, vigilance, and above all of listening. The hesychast, the person who has attained hesychia, inner stillness or silence, is par excellence the one who listens."[78] The importance of these times of silence and solitude is in listening to what God is saying to us. Prayer is a form of spiritual conversation, and the part that so often eludes us is the listening.

Fasting

Fasting, as St. John Chrysostom points out, is "abstinence not only from food but from sin . . . the fast should be kept, not by the

---

77. Ware, *The Inner Kingdom*, 91.
78. Meyendorff, *St. Gregory Palamas*, 25.

mouth alone, but also by the eye, the ear, the feet, the hands and all the members of the body."[79] This is an echo of the type of fast approved of by the Lord in Isaiah 58:6–12 with the addition of many blessings such as in verse 8 where it says,

> Then your light will break forth like the dawn,
> and your healing will quickly appear;
> then your righteousness will go before you,
> and the glory of the Lord will be your rear guard.

Bishop Kallistos Ware tells us that "fasting, then, is valueless or even harmful when not combined with prayer." He goes on to say that fasting should be combined with the triad of prayer, the sacraments, and acts of compassion. All of these actions are designed by God to lead us into greater intimacy with both him and with our fellow man. Acts of compassion have been connected to fasting since the second century in the church and should be a part of our dependence on God.[80]

It should be noted here that fasting was a normative part of Christian spiritual discipline from very early in the life of the church. The early church fasted on Wednesdays and Fridays to set themselves apart from the Jewish days of fasting. Fasting, however, was clearly a part of the Jewish tradition taken over by the church—a routine that continued to be observed even when the church became dominated by gentiles in the second and third centuries CE.[81]

Fasting should not be done in a mindset of spiritual pride but in obedience to the teachings of Scripture. We should not let any but those closest to us even know that we are fasting. We should not act as if we are fasting by looking downcast or gloomy (Matt 6:16, 18). The Lenten season, the time of fasting, is not one of gloom but of joyfulness.[82] It is a time of reordering our priorities,

---

79. Chrysostom, *Statutes Homily III*.
80. Mother Mary and Ware, *Lenten Triodion*, 4.
81. See St. Nikodemos, "Concerning Fasting on Wednesday and Friday," http://orthodoxinfo.com/praxis/exo_fasting.aspx.
82. Mother Mary and Ware, *Lenten Triodion*, 22.

Spiritual Tools

remembering God in our daily lives, and cleansing our will, rendering us ready for spiritual growth. Lent is called the "springtime" of the Christian year because it is the type of spring cleaning that leads to our continued renewal up to the great feast of the resurrection, Easter.[83]

Dallas Willard said, "Full participation in the life of God's Kingdom and in the vivid companionship of Christ comes to us only through appropriate exercise in the disciplines for life in the spirit."[84] This time of discipline is part of the Great Lent. The purpose of all of the spiritual disciplines is "the transforming of the whole person [body, soul, and spirit] into the likeness of Jesus."[85] We must, however, remember that by themselves the spiritual disciplines can do nothing; they can only get us to the place where something can be done. The inner righteousness we seek is not something that is poured on our heads. God has given us the disciplines of the spiritual life as the means by which we place ourselves where he can bless us.[86]

St. John Climacus calls Lent a season of "joy-creating sorrow."[87] Let us, during this season, seek to remember and prepare for the celebration of the resurrection. Let us act on those needed changes in our lives and take time to focus on what we should do better as well as on what we should do without. Here are some ideas of the kind of things that you can do during Lent and at other times of fasting that can have a powerful impact on your walk with the Lord.

---

83. Mother Mary and Ware, *Lenten Triodion*, 30.
84. Willard, *The Spirit of the Disciplines*, 166.
85. Mother Mary and Ware, *Lenten Trisagion*, 10.
86. Foster, *Celebration of Discipline*, 21.
87. John Climacus, *Ladder of Divine Ascent*, Step 7:9.

Three types of fasting:

COMPLETE FAST—LONG (MORE THAN A DAY OR TWO)

Eating no food. If you are going to do a complete fast, drink lots of liquids; anything else is not healthy.

COMPLETE FAST—BY MEAL

This is a fast where one does not eat a meal or two per day. In both the Eastern and Western traditions, this is the most common type of fasting. As in the above, it is very important to drink lots of liquids during even this short-term fasting.

PARTIAL FAST—BY TYPE OR QUANTITY.

You can fast from certain types of food such as meat, bread, sweets, etc. It is this type of fast that has become very popular in the West. It is based on the fast described in Daniel 10 where the prophet eats a simple diet as opposed to his usual more varied one. In the fast of quantity you can eat any type of food you wish but limit the amount that you eat. In all fasting, it is good, according to the church fathers, to leave the table hungry for more.

Cautionary Note: If you suffer from physical problems such as diabetes, high blood pressure, hypoglycemia, etc. please do not fast unless you check first with your doctor. Please be safe whenever you fast.

Biblical Fasting

In the Bible, fasting was done for three main reasons. The first is part of the mourning process at the death of a relative, friend, or national hero (1 Sam 31:13; 2 Sam 1:12; 3:35; 12:16, 21–23; 1 Chr 10:12).

Second, fasting was often enjoined or commanded during times of crisis (Exod 24:18; 34:28; Lev 16:29, 31; 23:27–32; Num

29:7; Deut 9:9, 18; 1 Sam 7:6; 2 Sam 1:12; 12:16; 1 Kgs 19:8; 2 Kgs 21:9; Esth 4:16; Ps 35:13; Jer 36:9; Ezek 8:21, 23; Dan 6:1; Joel 1:14; 2:12–13; Acts 27:9, 33–34).

Lastly, fasting was a voluntary act used to deal with sin or as a spiritual discipline. In this later form it was often associated with other forms of self-denial (Deut 9:18; 1 Sam 7:6; Neh 9:1; Jer 36:6; Dan 9:3; Matt 17:21; Acts 14:23).[88]

There are many great examples of fasting in the Old Testament, and in the New Testament we also have examples in the lives of Anna (Luke 2:37), Cornelius (Acts 10:30), Paul (2 Cor 6:5; 11:27), and, of course, Jesus (Matt 4:2; Mark 1:12–13; Lk 4:1–2).

The Power and Benefits of Fasting

The discipline of fasting is not just abstaining from food. It is a discipline whose goal is both mastery of the body and "recognizing our utter dependence upon God by finding in him a source of sustenance beyond food."[89] When we fast, we received greater spiritual power in our prayers (Matt 17:21, KJV).

My favorite example of fasting in the Bible is that of Daniel. He was a man of prayer and regularly fasted during times of prolonged prayer (Dan 9:3). He also had great influence in heaven when he prayed and fasted, even when it was only a partial fast (Dan 10:1–14).

Jesus, our greatest example of fasting, went into the wilderness to fast and pray before his great trial with Satan. We usually miss the fact that the wilderness where Jesus fasted and prayed was a place of strengthening for him. He was physically weakened by not eating but made spiritually ready for battle. He was preparing himself for the great struggle with his adversary and the disciplines of prayer and fasting gave him this added spiritual strength.

Fasting is not a discipline which can be utilized by all Christians. There are physical and medical conditions that may either

---

88. Belden, H. A. G., "Fasting," NBD 373.
89. Willard, *The Spirit of the Disciplines*, 59.

limit its use or make it impossible to practice. For those who can, however, it is a great source of intimacy with God. We learn in fasting to rely completely on his "bread" for our life. We are encouraged by the Scriptures to fast in both full (abstaining from food and sometimes from food and drink) and partial fasts (abstaining from certain foods). The point of fasting is to increase our intimacy with the Lord, not to lose weight. Use your times of fasting to pray, study, and grow closer to the Lord.

Evangelism

Evangelism is often a very misunderstood subject. It is a critical part of discipleship since, through it, people can be led by the Holy Spirit into the kingdom. There are basically three parts to evangelism. There is the proclamation, the outward manifestation of the kingdom in the spoken word, the lifestyle of the believer, and the manifestations of the Holy Spirit. We are clearly responsible for the first two. Sometimes we have overemphasized the proclaiming over lifestyle. We have also tended to underestimate the work of the Holy Spirit in this process.

In my lifetime, evangelism has meant preaching the gospel to an audience regardless of size. It has also meant person to person sharing of the gospel, small group Bible studies, and the like. Please let me be clear. These are all valid methods of spreading the good news, but there are also other methods, not talked about much, which include prayer and even martyrdom.

We must free ourselves from the wrong assumption that the key to evangelism is somehow tied to method. It is not. We are called to make disciples, and the first step is always the saving faith of the one who would be a disciple. We are called to act in this process, but the results are not in our control. As in all things, the main player in the process is the Holy Spirit. Our job is obedience to Christ's command to "be my witnesses" (Acts 1:8). Therefore, we are to witness using the means provided to us by the Holy Spirit.

When I was growing up, there was a lot of both encouragement and pressure to witness to someone every day. And even though everyone is not gifted as an evangelist, everyone in the kingdom is called to be a witness (Matt 28:18–20). This, however, should be a natural part of disciple-making and not a guilt trip based on the current preferred method. Evangelism can't be overemphasized but I am concerned that the rest of discipleship has been neglected. We have, in the West, made the primary goal of the church to bring people into a right relationship with God through acknowledgment of sin, repentance, and faith in the work of Jesus on the cross to open our way to salvation. Where we have erred is that we have made being saved the goal of the process.

The emphasis was skewed toward salvation, leaving Christians somewhat confused as to what should happen next, the focus being too narrow. In the last twenty-five years, I found a depth of spirituality that was light-years removed from my experience. People like Lewis, Murray, Bounds, Ironside, Moody, Luther, Calvin, and many other Protestant writers taught both an intellectual/theological foundation from the Scriptures and a deep spiritual understanding of discipleship that I had rarely seen exhibited in the churches I was part of. Added to that was the monastic tradition and the church fathers, both Catholic and Orthodox, all of whom, to one degree or other, offered an element of the Christian experience that spoke so powerfully to the whole arena of becoming like Christ. Most of this book comes from the realization that our purpose on earth and beyond is all about becoming what we were created to be—imitators of our Creator, or becoming "Christlike." This understanding has changed my whole way of thinking. If this is the goal of discipleship, then it must necessitate change and inform all of what we call the "Christian life."

Journaling

How to Get Started?

A spiritual journal is no mere exercise in discipline. It is a way to keep your thoughts, experiences, prayers, and their answers close to you to be remembered and meditated upon. This is a record of your unique relationship with God. Philosophers and educators have told us for centuries that knowledge is not achieved until it is thought about, broken down, associated with other ideas, and applied to the one doing the thinking. We also know that knowledge, when it is matured by formal education, life experience, and intimacy with God, can become wisdom. And wisdom is necessary in all times and in all places.

The best way that I have found to start a journal is to just start; just do it. Keeping a journal helps us to examine our walk with the Lord, reflect on what he has taught us, and consider how we think about the world around us. The issues that concern all of us are an important part of the spiritual disciplines. A journal is a living, spiritual history. It is never a mere exercise.

What to Include?

I suggest that you include significant experiences in your life even if they seem to have little relation to things "spiritual." You may see spiritual meaning in the most mundane events but usually at a distance or over a period of time. It is also a good idea to reread your journal on a regular basis. It's hard to know where you are going without knowing your past.

Break your journal down into several parts. From front to back, I keep a running journal of the events, concerns, prayers, etc. of each day. In the back of your journal keep some of the following:

- Bible insights
- Prayers
- Insights from the books, events, friends, parents, spouse, etc.

My journal also contains photos, clippings, or any other visual images that are important to me, and I refer to them often. Sometimes I just keep pictures of the people that I am praying for so that I can more clearly focus on them and their needs during prayer.[90]

90. Klug, *How to Keep a Spiritual Journal*, 2.

Spiritual Tools

Using the Tools of the Digital Age

Several years ago I would have scorned the idea that I would use a computer to write in my journal. I was into keeping a permanent record in something that felt substantial. I wrote in finely bound, fine art paper journals with a fountain pen. While this is perfectly acceptable, I found that there were times when I wanted to write and could not find my journal. I sat down at the computer and discovered something wonderful. When I typed, I could record my thoughts almost as fast as I thought them. It wasn't the desire for speed so much as the realization that I had handicapped myself with the medium I used to write in my journal. I was missing out on all that I had experienced simply because I couldn't get it down while it was still in my head. I don't know if you are like me. I have a great memory, it's just short. So I encourage you to try writing in your journal on the computer. I find a laptop to be a great tool for this purpose.

Original Prayers

Revival Prayer

Gracious Father, we have taken you for granted,
We sit idle when we are meant to be on fire.
Revive us, Lord, empower us to seek your face,
To seek to be conformed to your image.
Rain down on us, we pray,
The power and presence of your Holy Spirit,
Lord, revive your church!

Teacher's Prayer

Dear Lord and giver of wisdom,
prepare my students to pursue learning
with all their hearts and minds.
In all that I do and all that I say,

let me be careful to do none harm.
Help me encourage my students
and, in so doing, aid them to
acquire wisdom as well as knowledge.
Help me to listen and give me the courage
to tackle their hard questions with them.
Help me live what I teach
and give me the courage
to acknowledge when they teach me.
Give me wisdom to know when
to stop talking and allow them
to learn for themselves.
Give me patience, I pray, when they don't understand
as fast as I think they should.
Let me remember that they are not here for me
but that I am here for them.
Let their best memory of me
be how much I cared for them
not just the information I presented. Amen.

The Church Fathers on Prayer

"For if the prayer of one or two possesses such power that Christ stands in the midst of them, how much more will the prayer of the bishop and of the whole Church, ascending up in harmony to God, prevail for the granting of all their petitions in Christ!"—Ignatius[91]

"Be not satisfied with knocking and seeking; for prayer is of all things indispensable to the knowledge of the things of God."—Origen[92]

"Let not one think, my fellow Christian that only priests and monks need to pray without ceasing and not laymen No, no; every

---

91. Lightfoot and Harper, *The Apostolic Fathers*, 88.
92. Origen, *Ep. Greg.* 3.

Christian without exception ought to dwell always in prayer."—Gregory Palamas[93]

"And we neither ought to pray to know the future, nor to ask for it as the reward of our discipline; but our prayer should be that the Lord may be our fellow-helper for victory over the devil."—Athanasius[94]

"Those who pray as well as work on the tasks they have to do, and combine their prayers with suitable activities, will be praying always . . . we consider the entire life of the saints as one long prayer."—Origen[95]

"None can believe how powerful prayer is, and what it is able to effect, but those who have learned it by experience."—Martin Luther[96]

"O Lord our God, grant us grace to desire you with our whole heart; that so desiring we may seek and find you; and so finding you we may love you; and loving you, may hate the sins from which you have redeemed us."—Anselm[97]

"O Lord, who hast mercy upon all, take away from me my sins, and mercifully kindle in me the fire of the Holy Spirit. Take away from me the heart of stone, and give me a heart of flesh, a heart to love and adore thee, a heart to delight in thee, to follow and enjoy thee, for Christ's sake."—Ambrose[98]

---

93. http://www.orthodoxchurchquotes.com/2014/04/02/st-gregory-of-palamas-let-not-one-think-my-fellow-christian-that-only-priests-and-monks-need-to-pray-without-ceasing/.

94. Athaniasius, *Life of St. Antony*, ch. 34.

95. Origen, *Or.* 32.

96. Jacobs et al, *Collected Works of Martin Luther*, "Of Prayer."

97. From Belief Net, https://www.beliefnet.com/prayers/catholic/comfort/grant-us-grace.aspx.

98. From Catholic Online, https://www.catholic.org/prayers/prayer.php?p=3082.

"In prayer we begin to see ourselves as God sees us and we see God as he is. In prayer we acknowledge that we are not in control."
—Simon Chan[99]

"There is a proper time for everything except prayer; as for prayer, its proper time is always."—Antiochus of Sabas[100]

"A man who does not pray is one who is content with his own condition. He wished to remain as he is and not be changed, renewed or saved. His life unconsciously changes from bad to worse."
—Matthew the Poor[101]

---

99. Chan, *Spiritual Theology*, 129.
100. Ware, *The Inner Kingdom*, 75.
101. Chan, *Spiritual Theology*, 15.

5

The Church

EACH OF US AS individual Christians is not running this race alone. As the author of Hebrews tells us, we are "surrounded by such a great cloud of witnesses" (Heb 12:1), who watch and encourage us. We are part of the history of the church. We have the examples of those who have come before. In growing up among Evangelicals, there was very little sense that we were part of a larger church. There was, in fact, a certain suspicion of other churches, even those within our own circles. We were, to a large extent, cut off from the rich heritage that we had even within the Protestant history of the church. Like many of my generation of Evangelicals, I began to see that there was a greater church out there whose writings and history were also mine. During the Protestant Reformation we went too far in the attempts to throw off the evils that had made their way into the church. In so doing, we missed much of the good that was still there. We missed out on a lot.

One of the great joys and benefits I have experienced from this revelation is the opening up of the writings of the church fathers. The early monastic struggles of St. Anthony, St. Basil, St. Pachomius, and St. Benedict have inspired me. The theological genius of the Gregories (Gregory of Nyssa and Gregory of Nazianzus), St. Augustine, and St. Thomas Aquinas have made me think in a way I never had before. The simple spirituality and depth of St. Aidan, St. Cuthbert, St. Columba, and St. Seraphim of Sarov made me want to emulate them. This not to mention the relative newcomers like Thomas Merton, Alexander Schmemann, N. T. Wright, and Herni Nouwen. I found that much of what I had experienced was common to many others. What had happened to them could help with my questions. I have come back much richer for the experience.

THE CHURCH YEAR

Season—Color

Advent (Advent 1–Christmas Eve)—(Violet/Blue)

Advent is from the Latin for "arrival" and is the beginning of the Christian year as a time of preparation for the Nativity of our Lord (Christmas). This preparation has a threefold meaning. We celebrate Jesus having come into our lives, we prepare for the incarnation that has its culmination at his Nativity, and we wait for his Second Coming.[1] Advent is a time of thanksgiving for the gift of the past and hope for the future. The liturgical color violet represents majesty and serves to herald the coming of the King of kings. Traditional during Advent is the lighting of the Advent wreath. The wreath consists of four violet candles and is constructed in the shape of a circle with evergreen. The evergreen represents immortality, life, and growth and the circle stands for eternity. On the first Sunday in Advent, one candle is lit, and the second Sunday, two candles, and so on. A fifth candle is often used on Christmas Eve to symbolize the coming of Christ. This white candle is called the "Christ Candle." The Advent season is one of family worship with readings from Luke chapters 1 and 2. During this season we also celebrate the ministry of John the Baptist.[2]

---

1. Webber, *Book of Family Prayer*, 50–53.

2. Webber, *Book of Family Prayer*, 54; Bradner, *Symbols of Church Seasons and Days*, 10.

Christmastide (December 25–January 5)—(White)

The Nativity of our Lord Jesus Christ is a time of renewal and hope. It is said that this feast was first introduced into the Christian year in place of the pagan feasts to the "Unconquered Sun." These pagan feasts were Christianized into the feast of the birth of the Sun of Righteousness since the day and month of Jesus' birth are unrecorded. The twelve days of Christmas begin with Christmas Day and end at Epiphany on January 6. One of the most popular symbols of the Christmas season is the Christmas tree. The Christmas tree, at some times in church history, has represented the trees of life and knowledge that were in the garden of Eden. In medieval passion plays, for example, the paradise tree was usually a juniper adorned with apples and was often identified with Christ. The Christmas season is also a celebration of the dying and rising in baptism.[3]

Epiphany (January 6–Shrove Tuesday)—(Green)

Epiphany means a "manifestation of God" and is a celebration of the incarnation (God becoming human). This celebration is even older than Christmas according to Clement of Alexandria (c. AD 200). Epiphany celebrates Christ being made known to the gentiles (non-Jews) represented by the magi (wise men). Three themes run throughout this season. First is the nativity, which emphasizes the adoration of Jesus by the magi. Second is the baptism of Jesus where the Spirit of God descended on him in the form of a dove. And third is the first miracle of turning water into wine at the wedding in Cana. Jesus' baptism is also celebrated on the first Sunday after Epiphany.[4]

---

3. Webber, *Book of Family Prayer*, 57–62; Bradner, *Symbols of Church Seasons and Days*, 15, 16.

4. Webber, *Book of Family Prayer*, 80–82; Bradner, *Symbols of Church Seasons and Days*, 15.

The Disciple's Handbook

Lent (Ash Wednesday–Holy Saturday)—(Violet)

The term "Lent" simply means "spring." Lent is a six-week period of spiritual discipline before Easter which begins on Ash Wednesday. Originally, Lent was a time where those seeking to enter the church spent time in preparation for baptism, which would take place at Easter. This was a time of reflection, repentance, and identification with the sufferings of Christ. Others in the church began to join in with those being baptized, seeing this season as an opportunity to renew their personal covenant with God. The ashes used during the Ash Wednesday service, often made from the palm fronds kept from the previous Palm Sunday, signify repentance for our sins and our complete identification with the suffering of Christ (Gen 3:19; Job 42:6).[5]

Lent begins a period of fasting and preparation for Holy Week. Week one of Lent focuses on the power of Christ over the works of Satan, week two on Christ as the "Lamb of God" (John 1:29), week three on the freedom of the Christian from the power of death, and week four on the death of Christ (John 12:24). The Lenten season emphasizes the impending death of Jesus on the cross, the hope of the resurrection, and the necessity of faith and trust in Christ. Parallels are drawn between the forty days of Lent and the forty days that Jesus was tempted in the wilderness.[6]

The entire worship of the church—our foundation and the center of our being—is Easter. The Christian year is a cyclical journey that always leads us back to Easter, the entrance to the kingdom of God. The purpose of Lent is to soften our hearts to the realities of the Holy Spirit as we hunger and thirst for greater communion with God. This is a period of quieting our hearts and minds before God so that we can grow into supernatural living.

There is also an aspect of Lent that, although not a typical part of this season, is still appropriate to it. In the Orthodox tradition,

---

5. Webber, *Book of Family Prayer*, 103–6.

6. Webber, *Book of Family Prayer*, 106–10; Bradner, *Symbols of Church Seasons and Days*, 35.

Saturday and Sunday are not fast days even in the Lenten season but are always feast days. The feasting is lessened during Lent, but it is still a time of rejoicing. We must not lose the constant understanding that all of our worship is post-Calvary. Our sin has been paid for on the cross and, therefore, even in the season of repentance we must not forget our obligation to give glory to God. In a sense, every day of our lives should be lived in the tension between Lent and Easter. We need to sorrow and repent of our sins every day. This is why the *Book of Common Prayer* has a confession of sin in both morning and evening prayer. We also need to rejoice and bring him the worship due his name for our salvation and his continual care for us. We are fragile, sinful human beings, but we are also "more than conquerors."

Eastertide (Easter–Pentecost)—(White)

Easter is the Christian Pascha in the Orthodox tradition, the celebration of the cross and the redemption found in the resurrection. The Venerable Bede, an English monk and historian, tells us that the term "Easter" in English had its origins in the names of the pagan goddess "Eastre or Eoste" whose festival was celebrated at the spring equinox. Easter is celebrated on the Sunday following the first full moon after the Spring equinox. Symbols of Easter emphasize Jesus on the cross. "INRI" is often used, which refers to the notice written by Pilate at the head of the cross: *Iesus Nazareus Rex Iudaeorum*, or "Jesus of Nazareth, King of the Jews."[7]

Monday through Maundy Thursday (derived from the Latin "mandatum" or "commandment," referring to the "new commandment" in John 13:34) marks the beginning half of Holy Week. It is a time of reflection on the last week in the life of Jesus. On Good Friday (where the liturgical color changes to black for the only time in the church year) we remember the death of Jesus on the cross. Holy Saturday was the final day of preparation for those seeking baptism. Baptism was usually done at midnight on Easter

---

7. Webber, *Book of Family Prayer*, 141–43; Bradner, *Symbols of Church Seasons and Days*, 49.

Sunday morning. On Easter Sunday we burst forth with the joyous tidings "He is risen!" to which all who hear are to respond, "He is risen indeed!" The Easter season is the fifty days from Easter to Pentecost and commemorates the resurrection, the ascension of Jesus, and the coming of the Holy Spirit.[8]

Pentecost (Pentecost–Transfiguration)—(Red)

Also called Whitsunday (or white Sunday, which represents the white robes of the newly baptized), Pentecost is the culmination of the Easter celebration and recognizes the coming of the Holy Spirit upon the church in Acts chapter 2. This celebration comes from the Jewish Festival of Weeks, one of the festivals celebrated annually by every Hebrew male. It was a harvest festival and a time of thanksgiving for the first fruits of the harvest (Exod 34:22). It also served as a reminder of the giving of the Law at Mt. Sinai. In Christian worship, it was equated with the coming of the Holy Spirit on the seventy elders in Numbers 11:24-30. Ten days prior to Pentecost, we celebrate the ascension of Jesus into heaven. The spirit of this season is the opposite of the Lenten season. It is a season of joyous celebration.[9]

Kingdomtide (Transfiguration–Advent 1)—(Green)

Kingdomtide is the season after Pentecost. It includes feasts such as Trinity Sunday, the Transformation, All Saints' and All Souls' Days, and Christ the King Sunday. This is the longest time in the Christian year. Teaching about the kingdom of God is central to this season, hence the name "kingdomtide." The liturgical color is green and represents the growth and development of the people

---

8. Webber, *Book of Family Prayer*, 126-30; Bradner, *Symbols of Church Seasons and Days*, 44, 45.

9. Webber, *Book of Family Prayer*, 150-61; Bradner, *Symbols of Church Seasons and Days*, 56.

The Church

of God. Bible readings during this season are from Acts through Revelation.[10]

Other Special Days

Trinity Sunday—(White)

The first Sunday after Pentecost is Trinity Sunday. Trinity Sunday begins the time of the year in the Christian calendar called "kingdomtide." This Sunday contemplates and celebrates the mystery of the triune nature of our Lord. The triangle is used during this season, symbolizing the Trinity.

Transfiguration (August 6)—(Green)

This celebration is based on the event recorded in the Gospels (Matt 17:1–8; Mark 9:2–8; Luke 9:28–36). Jesus takes James, Peter, and John up the mountain, where he begins to glow with supernatural radiance. Jesus is joined by Moses (representing the Law) and Elijah (expected to come before the messiah and representing the prophets). It is one of two times when we see the Trinity together in the New Testament.[11] The other is the baptism of Jesus (Matt 3:16, 17).

All Saints' Day (November 1)—(Red)

This is the day that we remember all those believers who have died, especially those who were martyrs for the faith (Rev 7:9).[12]

---

10. Webber, *Book of Family Prayer*, 167.
11. Bradner, *Symbols of Church Seasons and Days*, 56.
12. Bradner, *Symbols of Church Seasons and Days*, 62.

All Souls Day (November 2)—(Red)

This is the day that we remember all who have died in Christ.[13]

Christ the King Sunday—(White)

This day celebrates the kingship of Jesus. It is the last Sunday in "kingdomtide" and the Sunday preceding the first Sunday of Advent. It begins the cycle of the Christian year all over again.[14]

Thanksgiving Day—(Red)

This is an American holiday celebrating our Puritan roots. We gather together as a community and give thanks to God for our country and God's blessings during the year (Ps 145:1–7).[15]

Personal Prayer List

- Family
- Parents
- Siblings
- Children
- Extended family
- Friends/coworkers
- Church needs
- Clergy
- Other leaders
- Individual needs

---

13. Bradner, *Symbols of Church Seasons and Days*, 64.
14. Bradner, *Symbols of Church Seasons and Days*, 64.
15. Bradner, *Symbols of Church Seasons and Days*, 64.

The Church

- Community leaders
  - Local
  - State
  - National
  - World

Bibliography

Achtemeier, Paul, ed. *Harper's Bible Dictionary* (HBD). San Francisco: Harper & Row, 1985.
Adam, David. *The Edge of Glory: Prayers in the Celtic Tradition.* Harrisburg, PA: Morehouse, 1987.
———. *The Open Gate: Celtic Prayers for Growing Spirituality.* London: SPCK, 1994.
Arnold, Duane W. H., trans. *Prayers of the Martyrs.* Grand Rapids: Zondervan, 1991.
Athanasius. *The Life of St. Antony.* New York: Newman, 1978.
Augustine. "Letter 169." http://www.newadvent.org/fathers/1102169.htm.
Bacovcin, Halen, trans. *The Way of a Pilgrim, and The Pilgrim Continues His Way.* New York: Doubleday, 1991.
Bede. *The Ecclesiastical History of the English People; The Greater Chronicle; Bede's Letter to Egbert.* Oxford World's Classics. Oxford: Oxford University Press, 1999.
Bercot, David W., ed. *A Dictionary of Early Christian Beliefs.* Peabody, MA: Hendrickson, 1998.
The Book of Common Prayer. Seabury, NY: 1977.
Boosalis, Harry. *Orthodox Spiritual Life according to St. Silouan the Athonite.* Waymart, PA: St Tikhon's Seminary, 2000.
Bouteneff, Vera, trans. *Father Arseny, 1893–1973: Priest, Prisoner, Spiritual Father; Being the Narratives Compiled by the Servant of God Alexander Concerning His Spiritual Father.* Crestwood, NY: St. Vladimir's Seminary, 1998.
Bradner, John. *Symbols of Church Seasons and Days.* Harrisburg, PA: Morehouse, 1977.
Breck, John. *Scriptures in Tradition.* Crestwood, NY: St. Vladimir's Seminary, 2001.
Brock, Sebastian, trans. *The Syriac Fathers on Prayer and the Spiritual Life.* Cistercian Studies Series 101. Kalamazoo, MI: Cistercian, 1988.
Carré, E.G., ed. *Praying Hyde.* South Plainfield, NJ: Bridge-Logos, 1982.
Cassian, John. *Conferences.* New York: Paulist, 1985.

Bibliography

Chadwick, Samuel. *The Collected Works of Samuel Chadwick.* Jawbone Digital, 2012. Kindle.
Chan, Simon. *Liturgical Theology: The Church as Worshiping Community.* Downers Grove: IVP Academic, 2006.
———. *Spiritual Theology: A Systematic Study of the Christian Life.* Downers Grove: IVP Academic,1998.
Chariton, Igumen. *The Art of Prayer: An Orthodox Anthology.* Boston: Faber and Faber, 1997.
Cherubim, Archimandrite. *A Manual of the Hours of the Orthodox Church.* Atica, Greece: Monastery of the Paraclete, 1993.
Chervin, Ronda De Sola. *Quotable Saints.* Ann Arbor, MI: Servant, 1992.
Chiffolo, Anthony F. *At Prayer with the Saints.* Liguori, MO: Liguori, 1998.
Chryssavgis, John. *Repentance and Confession in the Orthodox Church.* Brookline, MA: Holy Cross Orthodox, 1990.
Chryssavgis, John, and Benedicta Ward. *In the Heart of the Desert: The Spirituality of the Desert Fathers and Mothers.* Bloomington, IN: World Wisdom, 2003.
Climacus, John. *The Ladder of Divine Ascent.* Edited by Colm Luibheld et al. Classics of Western Spirituality. New York: Paulist, 1982.
Coleman, Richard. Unpublished Sermon. St. Michael's Chattanooga, TN, 10/8/2000.
———. Unpublished Sermon. St. Michael's Chattanooga, TN, 6/13/2010.
Coniaris, Anthony M. *Philokalia: The Bible of Orthodox Spirituality.* Minneapolis: Light and Life, 1998.
Cummings, Charles. *Monastic Practices.* Cistercian Studies Series. Kalamazoo, MI: Cistercian, 1986.
The Customary of the Society of St. Seraphim of Sarov. Phoenix: Society of St. Seraphim of Sarov, 2002.
Douglas, J.D., ed. *New Bible Dictionary* (NBD). Wheaton, IL: Tyndale, 1962.
Elder Joseph of Vatopaidi. *Obedience is Life.* Mount Athos, Greece: The Holy Great Monastery of Vatopaidi, 2003.
Finney, Charles. *Power from on High.* London: Victory, 1957.
First English Prayer Book. New York: Morehouse, 1999.
Fitzgerald, William J. *A Contemporary Celtic Prayer Book.* Chicago: ACTA, 1998.
Forest, Jim. *Praying with Icons.* New York: Orbis, 2008.
Fosdick, Harry Emerson. *The Meaning of Prayer.* New York: Association, 1917.
Foster, Richard J. *Celebration of Discipline.* Rev. ed. New York: Harper San Francisco, 1988.
Fry, Timothy, ed. *The Rule of St. Benedict.* Collegeville, MN: Liturgical, 1981.
Gillet, Lev. *The Jesus Prayer.* Crestwoord, NY: St. Vladimir's Seminary, 2018.
Hallesby, Ole. *Prayer.* Minneapolis, MN: Augsburg, 1941.
Hausherr, Irénée. *Spiritual Direction in the Early Christian East.* Grand Rapids: Cistercian, 1990.

Bibliography

Herman of Alaska Brotherhood. *Our Thoughts Determine Our Lives.* Translated by Ana Smilianic. Platina, CA: Herman of Alaska Brotherhood, 2011.

Hester, David. "The Jesus Prayer." https://store.ancientfaith.com/the-jesus-prayer-by-fr-david-hester/.

Holmes, Augustine. *A Life Pleasing to God: The Spirituality of the Rules of St. Basil.* Kalamazoo, MI: Cistercian, 2000.

Hopko, Thomas. *The Orthodox Faith.* Vol. 4, *Spirituality.* New York: OCA Dept. of Religious Education, 1984.

Iskander, Athanasius. *Practical Spirituality according to the Desert Fathers.* Kitchener, Ontario: St. Mary's Coptic Orthodox Church, 2005. Kindle.

Jacobs, C. M., et al., trans. *The Collected Works of Martin Luther.* E-artnow, 2018. Kindle.

Johnson, Luke Timothy. *Creed: What Christians Believe and Why It Matters.* New York: Image, 2004.

Kadloubovsky, E., and G. E. H. Palmer. *Writing from the Philokalia on Prayer of the Heart.* Boston: Faber and Faber, 1992.

Klug, Ronald. *How to Keep a Spiritual Journal.* Minneapolis: Augsburg, 1993.

Lake, John. *The Collected Works of John C. Lake.* Jawbone Digital, 2013. Kindle.

Law, William. *A Serious Call to a Devout and Holy Life.* Grand Rapids: Eerdmans, 1966.

Liddell, Eric. *The Disciplines of the Christian Life.* Escondido, CA: ChristianBooks, 1985.

Lightfoot, Joseph Barber, and John Reginald Harmer, trans. *The Apostolic Fathers.* Grand Rapids: Baker, 1989.

Manss, Virginia, and Mary Frohlich, eds. *The Lay Contemplative: Testimonies, Perspectives, Resources.* Cincinnati, OH: Franciscan Media, 2000.

Mantzarides, Giorgios. *Orthodox Spiritual Life.* Brookline, MA: Holy Cross Orthodox, 1994.

A Manual of Eastern Orthodox Prayers. Crestwood, NY: St. Vladimir's Seminary, 1991.

Marett-Crosby, Anthony, ed. *The Benedictine Handbook.* Collegeville, MN: Liturgical, 2003.

Mark the Monk. *Counsels on the Spiritual Life.* Vol.1 translated by Tim Vivian, vol. 2 translated by Tim Vivian and Augustine Casiday. Crestwood, NY: St. Vladimir Seminary, 2009. Kindle.

Markides, Kyriacos. *The Mountain of Silence.* New York: Doubleday, 2001.

Martimort, Aimé Georges, trans, et al. *The Liturgy and Time.* Collegeville, MN: Liturgical, 1983.

Mathews-Green, Frederica. *At the Corner of East and Now.* New York: Penguin Putnam, 1999.

Matthew the Poor. *Orthodox Prayer Life: The Interior Way.* Crestwood, NY: St. Vladimir's Seminary, 2003.

McConkey, James H. *The Surrendered Life.* SolidChristianBooks.com, 2015. Kindle.

McGuckin, John Anthony. *The Orthodox Church.* Malden, MA: Blackwell, 2011.

Bibliography

Merton, Thomas. *Contemplative Prayer*. New York: Random House, 1971.

———. *New Seeds of Contemplation*. New York: New Directions, 1972.

Meyendorff, John. *Byzantine Theology*. Fordham University Press, 1979.

———. *St. Gregory Palamas and Orthodox Spirituality*. Crestwood, NY: St. Vladimir's Seminary, 1997.

Monk Moses. "Prayer as an Important Aspect of Our Spiritual Life." https://www.goarch.org/-/prayer-as-an-important-aspect-of-our-spiritual-life.

Monk of the Eastern Church. *The Jesus Prayer*. Crestwood, NY: St. Vladimir's Seminary, 1987.

Mother Mary, and Kallistos Ware, trans. *The Lenten Triodion*. South Canaan, PA: St. Tikhon's Seminary, 2002.

Murray, Andrew. *With Christ in the School of Prayer*. New Kensington, PA: Whitaker House, 1981.

My Prayer Book. St. Louis, MO: Concordia, 1983.

Nicozisin, George. *The Orthodox Church: A Well-Kept Secret*. Minneapolis: Light and Life, 1997.

Niebuhr, H. Richard. *Christ and Culture*. New York: Harper Torchbooks, 1951.

Nun Macaria. *Spiritual Treasures in Filthy Rags*. Crestwood, NY: Theosis, 2016.

Olson, Mark. *John Wesley's "A Plain Account of Christian Perfection."* Annotated ed. 2010. Kindle.

Painter, Rick. Unpublished Sermon. St. Michael's Chattanooga, TN, 8/2/2002.

Palmer, G. E. H., et al., trans. *The Philokalia*. Boston: Faber and Faber, 1995.

Pelikan, Jaroslav. *The Emergence of the Catholic Tradition (100–600)*. The Christian Tradition 1. Chicago: University of Chicago Press, 1971.

Pennington, M. Basil. *Lectio Divina*. New York: Crossroad, 1998.

Phillips, Ron. *Radical Choices: Choosing to Change*. Cleveland: Pathway, 2005.

A Prayer Book for Orthodox Christians. Boston: Holy Transfiguration Monastery, 2000.

Roberts, Alexander, et al., eds. *The Works of Origen*. 2011. Kindle. https://www.amazon.com/Works-Origen-Principiis-Letters-Contents-ebook/dp/B0060GCL5U.

Shuttleworth, Mark. *Theosis: Partaking of the Divine Nature*. Ben Lomond, CA: Conciliar, 2005.

Staniloae, Dumitru. *Orthodox Spirituality*. Waymart, PA: St. Tikhon's Seminary, 2003.

Symonds, Kevin. *Pope Leo XIII and the Prayer to St. Michael*. Preserving Christian, 2018. Kindle.

Unknown Christian. *The Kneeling Christian*. Grand Rapids: Zondervan, 1929.

Ward, Benedicta, trans. *The Sayings of the Desert Fathers*. Kalamazoo, MI: Cistercian, 1975.

Ware, Timothy (Kallistos). *The Inner Kingdom*. Crestwood, NY: St. Vladimir's Seminary, 2001.

———. *The Orthodox Church*. New York: Penguin, 1997.

———. *The Power of the Name*. Oxford: SLG, 1999.

BIBLIOGRAPHY

Webber, Robert E. *Ancient-Future Evangelism: Making Your Church a Faith-Forming Community.* Grand Rapids: Baker, 2003.

———. *Ancient-Future Time: Forming Spirituality through the Christian Year.* Grand Rapids: Baker, 2004.

———. *The Book of Family Prayer.* New York: Thomas Nelson, 1986.

———. *The Divine Embrace.* Grand Rapids: Baker, 2006.

———. *The Prymer: The Prayer Book of the Medieval Era Adapted for Contemporary Use.* Boston: Paraclete, 2000.

Wesley, John. *How to Pray.* Uhrichsville, OH: Barbour, 2007.

Wilberforce, Basil. *Following on to Know the Lord.* New York: Hodder and Stoughton, 1904.

Wilberforce, William. *Real Christianity.* Portland, OR: Multnomah, 1982.

Willard, Dallas. *The Spirit of the Disciplines.* San Francisco: Harper San Francisco, 1991.

Wright, N. T. *The Day the Revolution Began.* New York: HarperOne, 2016.

———. *Following Jesus: Biblical Reflections on Discipleship.* Grand Rapids: Eerdmans, 1994.

www.ingramcontent.com/pod-product-compliance
Lightning Source LLC
Chambersburg PA
CBHW070930160426
43193CB00011B/1638